T5-BBP-010

THE HERMITAGE

Aurora Art Publishers. Leningrad. 1976

THE HERMITAGE

ROOM-TO-ROOM GUIDE

TEXT BY O. PERSIANOVA

TRANSLATED BY JOHN S. HEYES

Third edition, revised

Э $\dfrac{80101\text{-}710}{023(01)\text{-}76}$ без объявления

The New Hermitage

The Hermitage ranks with the very finest of the world's art museums. It contains more than two and a half million works of art representing different ages, countries and peoples.

The history of the Hermitage is closely connected with that of the buildings which house the present-day museum. The Winter Palace and the three buildings of the Hermitage, conventionally called the Small Hermitage, the Old Hermitage and the New Hermitage, and united by a series of covered passage-ways, form one of the most superb architectural ensembles in Leningrad.

The Winter Palace. The Winter Palace was built between 1754 and 1762 by Bartolommeo Rastrelli (1700—1711) in magnificent Baroque style. The inside of the Palace has been reconstructed several times: during the 1780s and 1790s by Giacomo Ouarenghi (1744—1817) and Ivan Starov (1744—1808) and in the first thirty years of the nineteenth century by such distinguished architects as Carlo Rossi (1775—1849) and Auguste Montferrand (1786—1858). In the winter of 1837 a fire broke out and burnt for three days, leaving nothing but charred walls. The restoration work under Vasily Stasov (1769—1848) and Alexander Briullov (1798—1877) was completed for the most part by the spring of 1839. The exterior was restored in the original, the majority of the interiors redecorated in late Classical style. For more than a century and a half the Winter Palace served as the residence of the tsars; then, for a short time, as the seat of the Provisional Government. Finally, after the Revolution, the Palace became a museum.

The Main Staircase of the Winter Palace. From the entrance hall on Palace Embankment we enter the Rastrelli Gallery, at the end of which the ceremonial staircase of the Winter Palace comes into view. High, well lit and sparkling with gilt and mirrors, the staircase was redesigned after the fire of 1837 by Vasily Stasov in keeping with the plan of Rastrelli, though with certain alterations. Stasov replaced the pillars of pink imitation marble with columns of grey granite from Serdobol (Karelia), and the gilded wooden handrail with a marble balustrade. On pedestals are the following alabaster statues: *Wisdom* and *Justice* by Terebenev, *Grandeur* and *Opulence* by Ustinov, *Fidelity* and *Equity* by Leppe, *Mercury* and *Mars* by Manuylov, and *The Muse* by Hermann. In the central recess on the lower landing stands the marble sculpture entitled *Allegory of the State (Sovereignty)* by an unknown eighteenth century sculptor. The eighteenth century ceiling portrays the gods on Olympus.

The Foundation of the Hermitage. The Hermitage is regarded as having been founded in the year 1764, when two hundred and twenty-five paintings were delivered to the Palace, having been bought for the Russian empress Catherine II from the Berlin merchant Gotzkowsky. After this, large consignments of paintings acquired at sales began to arrive one after the other from abroad: the Brühl collection from Saxony in 1769, Crozat's, bought in France in 1722, the Walpole gallery from England and several others. Prints, sculptures, carved stones, coins and medals, tapestries, jewellery, in addition to paintings, gave the Hermitage collections exceptional diversity. The treasures of the palace museum, which is what the Hermitage was at that time, were regarded as the personal possession of the Empress, and very few people were allowed to visit the collection. In one of her letters Catherine wrote, referring to the riches of the Hermitage: "Only the mice and I can admire all this..."

The Winter Palace from the Neva Embankment

The Small Hermitage. Between 1764 and 1767, according to a plan made by Yury Velten (1730—1801) and Jean-Baptiste-Michel Vallin de la Mothe (1729—1800), a building of smallish proportions was erected adjacent to the Winter Palace. This became known as the "Hermitage" (from the French *ermite*, a recluse; hence "hermitage", the abode of a recluse, a place of solitude), which was used by Catherine for unofficial receptions. The art collections were accommodated in two galleries adjoined by the Hanging Garden which was laid out on the roof of the Palace stables. In 1856 the architect Andrey Stakenschneider (1802—1865) designed the still existing Pavilion Hall in what had been some small rooms built during the time of Catherine. At the present time the Pavilion Hall contains an excellent collection of eighteenth and nineteenth century Italian mosaics—for example the mosaic tables *The Bottom of the Sea, A Day in Rome*. A floor mosaic, a copy of an ancient Roman original now preserved in the Vatican museum, was completed

The Small Hermitage

between 1847 and 1851 by artists who had studied in Rome. Another notable feature of the Hall is the "Peacock" clock, the work of James Coxe, an eighteenth century English watchmaker. The complex mechanism, concealed beneath a mound above which stands the trunk of a tree, sets in motion, when the clock strikes, the figures of a peacock, an owl and a cockerel. A small revolving dial, set in the cap of a toadstool, shows the time.

The Old Hermitage was built in 1787 by the architect Yury Velten to accommodate the ever growing collection of works of art. In the nineteenth century, rooms on the first floor, which now contain an exhibition of thirteenth to sixteenth century Italian art, were redecorated by Stakenschneider as additional Palace premises, and this décor has been preserved up to the present day.

The Growth of the Collection. In the course of time the collections were enriched by relics of Greek and Scythian culture, unearthed during excavations on ancient burial mounds in southern Russia. Thus was begun the world-famous collection of Scythian antiquities and of relics from ancient towns on and around the northern Black Sea coast. The purchase of the best items from the collection of the Marquis of Campana in Rome in 1861 facilitated the creation of a department devoted to the art of classical antiquity. At the same time, though not so intensively, a collection was accumulated of items of oriental culture. Throughout the nineteenth century up to the beginning of the twentieth the Hermitage collections were further enlarged by the acquisition of works of art from ancient Egypt and Mesopotamia, individual specimens of Sassanian and Byzantine silver, Coptic fabrics, Syrian vessels, oriental

The Hanging Garden

weapons, etc. There was an increase in the number of works of Western European art: in 1814 a large part of the Malmaison gallery was bought from the empress Josephine (Napoleon's first wife), and in 1815 the collection of the Amsterdam banker Coesvelt was added. The collection of the Spanish minister Godoy was acquired in 1836, and in 1850 that of the Venetian Barbarigo family among others. Leonardo da Vinci's *The Litta Madonna* was purchased in Milan in 1866, and *The Benois Madonna* in St Petersburg in 1914, and Raphael's *Conestabile Madonna* in Perugia in 1870. A collection of medieval works of art belonging to A. Bazilevsky was bought in Paris in 1884. The last major purchase before the Revolution was made in 1915, when the museum acquired, after the death of the famous Russian geographer and traveller P. Semionov-Tyanshansky, his large collection of Dutch and Flemish paintings.

The New Hermitage. Between 1842 and 1851 Yefimov (1799—1851) carried out the construction, according to the design of the Munich architect Leo Klenze (1784—1864), of a special museum building—the New Hermitage, the entrance to which, from the present-day Khalturin Street, is adorned by a portico with grey granite atlantes, five metres high (a little over 16 ft.), the work of A. Terebenev (1812—1859).

The ceremonial opening of the Imperial Hermitage took place in 1852. For a long time, however, tickets enabling the bearer to visit the museum were issued by a court office; admission was granted only to those wearing military uniform or tail-coat. Only in the late nineteenth century did admission to the museum become relatively easy.

The Hermitage after the Revolution. In October 1917 the Winter Palace was witness to a great historic event. From the morning of November 7th (October 25th O.S.) detachments of Red Guards and revolutionary units of soldiers and sailors rushed from the headquarters of the Revolution at Smolny to the Winter Palace, where the ministers of the counter-revolutionary Provisional Government took refuge under the protection of the officer cadets and shock troops. During the night of November 7th the Winter Palace was taken by storm.

In spite of the difficult conditions of civil war, foreign intervention and post-war economic disruption, the Soviet government, under the personal guidance of Lenin, took vigorous measures towards preserving the cultural legacy of the past. In October 1918 a special decree was issued

The Pavilion Hall

by the Council of People's Commissars concerning the preservation and registering of works of art and relics of antiquity.

During the years of Soviet power the scope of the Hermitage collections has been enlarged more then fourfold. Among the works acquired are the finest items from the Anichkov Palace, the suburban palaces of Peterhof and Gatchina, and from the private picture galleries of the Youssupovs, Stroganovs, Shuvalovs and Sheremetevs requisitioned by the state after the Revolution, and from the galleries of the Moscow collectors, Shchukin and Morozov, and a number of others. For the purposes of acquiring works of art and ancient relics expeditions were made on several occasions to the Caucasus, Central Asia and other parts of the country, and many valuable items have been, and are still being bought from private individuals by a special purchasing commission. Lastly, there are excavations systematically conducted by Soviet scholars, and these represent inexhaustible sources for the enrichment of the museum: It eventually became possible to create new departments — departments devoted to the history of Russian culture, to prehistoric culture, and to the culture and art of the peoples of the East. Besides, a scientific department was organized, its work involving tours of the musum and lectures. A fundamental rearrangement of all the exhibitions on the basis of the Marxist-Leninist approach to history made it possible to show, in the first-class items of the Hermitage, the history of world art and culture in its natural, successive stages of development.

The Hermitage during the War of 1941—45. In the very first days of the war all valuable items were carefully packed and made ready for evacuation. 1,118,000 exhibits were dispatched to the safety of the Urals; the remainder, largely decorative objects, were put into the cellars of the Winter Palace. Bombing attacks and artillery fire caused considerable damage to the buildings of the Hermitage; thus, as a result of direct hits, the famous portico of the New Hermitage with the atlantes was damaged, as well as several rooms in the Winter Palace. Glass was blown out of the windows, and paintings on the ceilings and walls, stucco work, gilt and inlaid floors all suffered from the dampness and cold. Even during the siege of Leningrad plans were made for the reconstruction work, which was begun immediately after the blockade was lifted. On November 8th, 1945, after an interval of four years, the doors of the Hermitage were again opened to visitors.

The Hermitage today. At present the collections of the Hermitage number 2,600,000 items. These include about 15,000 paintings, 12,000 sculptures, 600,000 prints and drawings, over 600,000 archaeological exhibits, 1,000,000 coins and medals, and 220,000 items of applied art. Four hundred rooms are open to the public.

Expressing its high regard for the services rendered by the museum staff in art education, the Presidium of the Supreme Soviet awarded the Hermitage the Order of Lenin in connection with the museum's two hundredth anniversary in 1964.

THE DEPARTMENT
OF RUSSIAN CULTURE

Rooms on the first floor of the Winter Palace contain the collections of the museum's youngest department—that devoted to the history of Russian culture, created in 1941. At present the department includes the following exhibitions: The Culture of Old Russia, 6th—15th centuries; The Culture of Muscovite Russia, 15th—17th centuries; Russian Culture, 1700—25; Russian Culture, 1740—1800; and Russian Culture, 1800—60. Included in the exhibition in the Department of Russian Culture are the state apartments of the Winter Palace, which have both artistic and historical significance.

The Memorial Room of Peter the Great (194) was decorated in 1833 by Auguste Montferrand. The walls are covered with crimson Lyons velvet, with two-headed eagles embroidered in silver, and upon a dais in the recess stands the throne of the Russian tsars. Above the throne there is a painting by the eighteenth century Italian artist Jacopo Amiconi portraying Peter the Great beside Minerva, the goddess of wisdom. Overhead on the side walls are two panels representing Peter in the battles of Lesnaya and Poltava. The room was restored in the original style after the fire of 1837 by the architect Vasily Stasov.

The Armorial Hall (195) was designed by Stasov after the fire. The pictures of the coats of arms and heraldic emblems of all the provinces of Russia, attached to bronze chandeliers, gave the name to the hall, which was intended for balls and receptions.

The 1812 Gallery (197) was designed in 1826 by Carlo Rossi and later restored by Stasov. On the walls hang more than three hundred portraits of generals engaged in the War of 1812, among them the portraits of Kutuzov (full length) and his companions-in-arms Bagration, Yermolov,

Rayevsky, Davydov and many others. The portraits were painted by the famous English artist George Dawe (1781—1829) who, with the assistance of the Russian painters Poliakov and Golike, worked in the Palace from 1819 to 1829 on the completion of the commissioned work. The equestrian portraits of Alexander I and his ally in the war with Napoleon, Frederick William III of Prussia, were painted by the German artist Franz Krüger (1797—1857), and that of the Austrian emperor Francis I, by the Austrian Peter Krafft (1780—1856).

At the time of the fire in 1837 the portraits were removed from the flames by guardsmen assisting in the rescue of the Palace treasures. One's attention is drawn to some empty frames filled with green taffeta. The inscriptions on the frames give the names and ranks of those who fell in battle and whose portraits it was not possible to reproduce.

The 1812 Gallery was eulogized by Pushkin as a monument to the glory of Russia.

The St George Hall (198), also known as the Large Throne Hall, is solemn and austere in appearance. It is decorated with white Carrara marble imported from Italy and gilded bronze. The parquet floor, made from sixteen different kinds of valuable wood, mirrors exactly the bronze ceiling pattern. Opposite the entrance to the room is a marble bas-relief, *St George Slaying the Dragon*, executed by the Italian sculptor Francesco del Nero after a drawing by Stasov, who designed the room in full (1842). In the St George Hall, which occupies eight hundred square metres (8,608 sq. ft.), there is a map of the Soviet Union made of semiprecious stones, standing on the same spot as the throne in former times. The map was executed by craftsmen from Leningrad and Sverdlovsk; it has twice been on view at world exhibitions—in 1937 in Paris, where it was awarded a Grand Prix, and in New York, in 1939. Beautiful and also of great precision, the map is made from forty-five thousand pieces of stone —jasper of various kinds, lapis lazuli, rhodonite, porphyry, etc.—and on the surface of the map, which covers an area of twenty-seven square metres (290 sq. ft.), the different physical features are shown in relief. The valleys are green, the mountain tops snow-white, the seas and oceans blue, and the contours of the mountain ranges brown. The diamonds of the hammer and sickle sparkle and gleam against the ruby star representing on the map the capital of the Soviet Union, Moscow.

The 1812 Gallery. Winter Palace

The Antechamber (192) leads to a suite of state rooms overlooking the Neva. Next to it is the **Great Hall (191)**, also known as the Ballroom which, with an area of over one thousand one hundred square metres (12,716 sq. ft.), is the largest room in the Palace. Nowadays the hall is used to house temporary exhibitions.

The Concert Hall of the Winter Palace (190) contains an exhibition entitled Russian Silverware: late 17th—early 20th centuries. The most noteworthy item in the exhibition is the tomb of Alexander Nevsky in the form of a sarcophagus, embellished with rich ornamentation and bas-reliefs depicting scenes fram the life of Alexander Nevsky, and with an ornamental pyramid bearing the figures of winged genii. On the shields which the genii hold in the hands are engraved lines by Mikhail Lomonosov, the eminent Russian poet and scientist, dedicated to Alexander

The Memorial Room of Peter the Great. Winter Palace

Nevsky and to this unusual work. The tomb was made in the middle of the eighteenth century at the St Petersburg Mint, and in all almost 1.5 tons of silver were used, obtained in the space of one year from the Kolyvan mines in the Altai region of west Siberia.

The Malachite Room (189), one of the most beautiful rooms in the Palace, designed in 1829 by A. Briullov, is notable for its malachite columns, pilasters and mantelpieces, executed in the technique known as Russian mosaic. In this technique the stone or metal base of an object was tiled with thin, carefully polished pieces of a rare, deep green stone obtained in the Urals. Over two tons of malachite were used on the decoration of the room.

The historical associations of the Malachite Room are full of interest. During the night of November 7th the last meeting of the counter-revolutionary Provisional Government took place here. Upon the storming of the Winter Palace the ministers took cover in the adjoining room, the **Private Dining-room (188)**, where they were arrested by the

The St George Hall. Winter Palace

revolutionaries. The Private Dining-room, designed in 1894 according to the plan of the architect Meltzer, still retains the appearance and atmosphere of those historic days.

The Culture of Old Russia:
6th—15th centuries
Rooms 143—150

The exhibition consists basically of material obtained in recent years by Soviet scholars during archaeological research on ancient Slavonic settlements and burial-grounds, and on old Russian towns.

Room 143. An important place is occupied in the exhibition by items found during excavations on the sites of eighth to tenth century Slavonic settlements—Novotroitsky (Sumy province), Borshevsky (Voronezh province), and the Monastyrishche site near the town of Romny. The

2

collections of agricultural implements and household utensils testify to the fact that the inhabitants of these settlements were engaged in agriculture, cattle-breeding, hunting and fishing. The existence of crafts is confirmed by an iron-smelting furnace of the ninth and tenth centuries discovered in the province of Vinnitsa near the village of Grigorovka. Interesting material has come from the Old Ladoga excavations, including some well preserved wooden objects—parts of a weaving-loom, a spindle, a comb for carding flax, oars and parts of a boat.

Exhibited in **room 144** are groups of objects which illustrate the way of life and the culture of rural communities in old Russia. The material in **room 145** is devoted to a display of urban culture, based upon the example of Old Ladoga and Belaya Vezha, important centres of trade and crafts from the tenth to twelfth century. Archaeological research on the latter was carried out between 1949 and 1951 in connection with the construction of the Volga-Don Canal.

Room 146. Weapons and armaments used by the Russian warrior —chain mail, the sword and the spear-heads found on the site of the Raikovetsky settlement near the town of Berdichev—are evidence of the heroic defence and the destruction of this small fortress-town during the invasion of Russian lands by the Tartar-Mongol hordes of Batu-Khan.

The exhibitions in **rooms 147—149** provide an introduction to the architecture, art and relics of writing of the tenth to thirteenth century. Of particular value are some frescoes and a mosaic floor from the church of the Mikhailovsko-Zlatoverkhy monastery in Kiev (early twelfth century). Examples of stone carving, used to embellish the façades of shrines and palaces, reflect the great mastery of the Russian builders and craftsmen, among whom the stone carvers of the Vladimir-Suzdal principality were particularly renowned. There is also some splendid jewellery, adorned with the most exquisite *cloisonné* enamel, granulation, filigree and niello. The "Tmutorokan Stone" is an ancient relic indicating the early development of writing in Russia. It is a large marble slab bearing the inscription of the Russian prince, Gleb, which speaks of the work, carried out in 1068, of measuring the distance between Korchev (Kerch) and Tmutorokan (Taman). A letter written on the bark of a birch-tree found during excavations at Pskov, denotes the growth of literacy during the twelfth century among the middle strata of urban society **(room 148)**.

The Private Dining-room. Winter Palace

The culture of Pskov and Novgorod is represented in the exhibits of **room 150**, which contains fragments of architectural ornamentation, a collection of icons, examples of craft work and various implements and articles of domestic life.

The Culture of Muscovite Russia:
15th—17th centuries
Room 151

The exhibition begins with archaeological material of the twelfth to seventeenth century found on excavation sites in Moscow. The fifteenth and sixteenth centuries are represented in the Hermitage by a limited number of items, reflecting but a few of the aspects of the cultural development of Muscovite Russia, a strong centralized state which had unified the various lands of Russia. Particularly deserving of attention are the fifteenth century icons *Scenes from the Life of St Nicholas of Zaraisk*, *Scenes from the Life of St Demetrius the Warrior*, *The Last Judgement*, a sixteenth century icon, and some details of architectural decoration and fragments of ornamented stone slabs. Among the examples of craft work are some specimens of sixteenth century silversmiths' art notable for the great skill with which they were made. Two works, *The Apostle* and *The*

Pendants. Gold, *cloisonné* enamel. Kiev, 12th century

Icon of St Nicholas.
Novgorod school,
13th century

Bible, by the first Russian printer, Ivan Fiodorov, indicate the development of printing in Russia (horizontal case near the window). The adjacent case contains hand-written and printed books dating from the seventeenth century—an alphabet book by Karion Istomin and a grammar by Melety Smotritsky, in which the traditional Church Slavonic texts are rendered less formal by the introduction of colloquial Russian forms. The visitor's attention will be aroused by the hand-written book, *Tituliarnik* (a book of titles), which is decorated with water-colour portraits of Russian grand princes, tsars, and also Western European monarchs. The *Tituliarnik* was commissioned by tsar Alexey Mikhailovich for the young Peter.

One of the most outstanding items in the exhibition is the map of Siberia, painted on cloth in 1698 by the scholar and geographer Remezov, who adhered to the system of Oriental cartographers and placed the south uppermost, the north at the bottom, the west on the right and the east on the left. The map amply conveys the peculiar features of this distant region, indicates the towns of Tobolsk, Irkutsk and Krasnoyarsk, and the settlements and nomad encampments of the Yakuts, Evenks and Chukchi.

The exhibition ends with a display of late seventeenth century art, in which of particular interest is the icon *St John the Winged Precursor* painted in 1689 by Tikhon Filatyev, a fine painter of the Moscow school.

Russian Culture: 1700—25
Rooms 152—161

Most of the items in the exhibition come from the memorial museum of Peter the Great (called Peter the Great's Study) founded shortly after his death and attached to the *Kunstkammer* (Cabinet of Curios) of the Academy of Sciences. Documents, engravings, books, instruments, tools and works of art all point to the important changes which took place in Russia as a result of reforms introduced by Peter. The successful development of the home industry may be represented by a silver bowl in the form of a small ship, made of silver obtained from the mines of Nerchinsk in Siberia, and by a salver of bronze from the copper works of Ekaterinburg. The armourer's workshops of Tula and Olonets, established during the reign of Peter, produced guns, pistols, mortars, and a cast-iron cannon bearing the inscription: "Olonets, 1711". There is also a large display of astronomical, artillery and navigational instruments connected with the creation of the Russian navy and artillery. Of further interest is a collection of various medical instruments. Numerous engravings commemorate important events during the Great Northern War, which lasted from 1700 until 1721. Teaching tables entitled *A New Method of Arithmetic, The Mirror of the Skies* and *A Picture Map of the World* remind us of the fact that following the reforms carried out by Peter, the whole system of education underwent a radical transformation and the so-called "Arithme-

CARLO BARTOLOMMEO
RASTRELLI.
Bust of Peter the Great

tic" schools (providing a general education) and special schools (navigational, artillery, medical) were organized. A printing press from the Senate printing office made in 1721 arouses considerable interest.

Displayed in **room 155** is a rare collection of duplicating lathes from Peter's own workshop, among them the large lathe designed by the talented mechanic Andrey Nartov (1693—1756). The details were painstakingly made by hand, and the lathe is complete with mechanical support.

In **room 156**, amongst articles turned on these lathes, is an ivory candelabrum, certain details of which were made by Peter himself. In the centre of the room stands the "Triumphal Column", a model of the monument which they intended to erect on one of the squares in St Petersburg to commemorate Russian victories in the Great Northern

War. The stem of the column consists of eight bronze cylinders with bas-relief scenes from land and sea battles, and the column is surmounted by a statue of Peter the Great, a copy of the wooden sculpture made by Carlo Bartolommeo Rastrelli (*c.* 1670—1744), the father of the great architect.

The display also includes certain memorial items, namely the uniform and hat worn by Peter on the day of the battle of Poltava, June 9th, 1709. In **room 157** are exhibited numerous objects of art and ornaments in ivory, metal and glass,which show the development   during Peter's time of the different branches of the applied arts.

Room 158 contains works of painting, sculpture, drawing and engraving. Notable for its great artistic merit is the bronze bust of Peter the Great created by the sculptor Carlo Bartolommeo Rastrelli in 1723. The facial expression, the impetuous turn of the head reveal the complex character of the tsar, his inflexible will, intellect and energy. On the breastplate an allegorical scene is depicted: Peter is carving from stone the figure of a woman wearing a royal crown, personifying the might of Russia. Engravings by the talented craftsman Alexey Zubov (1682—after 1744), outstanding among which is the Petersburg Panorama (1716), present the topographical record of the city on the Neva during the first ten years of its existence. In a horizontal case near the window is a collection of portrait miniatures on enamel, among them a group portrait of Peter and members of his family, the work of the famous artist Musikiysky (1670/71—after 1739).

Displayed in **room 159** are items of furniture and decorative objects from the first quarter of the eighteenth century, among them the tapestry, *Peter the Great at the Battle of Poltava*, indicating the achievements of the Russian craftsmen of the St Petersburg tapestry workshop which was set up in 1717.

Occupying pride of place in **room 160** is the effigy representing Peter seated in an armchair. The statue was created by Carlo Bartolommeo Rastrelli in life size (Peter was 6 ft. 8 in. tall) immediately after the death of the tsar. Wax impressions were made of the face, hands and feet, the body was cut from wood, and the wig, according to legend, was made from Peter's own hair. The figure is dressed in the robes worn by the tsar at the coronation of Catherine I in 1724.

LOMONOSOV. Portrait of Peter the Great. Mosaic. 1755—57

Russian Culture: 1740—1800
Rooms 162—174

Room 163 contains material devoted to the work and activities of Mikhail Lomonosov (1711—1765). As a result of many experiments Lomonosov discovered the composition of smalt and revived the art of mosaic, which had flourished in old Russia. There are five mosaics on display, created in the workshop of which he himself was master. Notable among these is the portrait of Peter the Great, Lomonosov's own work. In the exhibition there are examples of Lomonosov's scientific and literary work and some astronomical instruments, manufactured in the workshop of the Academy of Sciences, to which he devoted much attention, all affording evidence of the many-sided talents of one of the eighteenth century's greatest scholars.

Examples of Russian painting, largely portraiture, which came into vogue on a large scale in the eighteenth century, are to be found in **rooms 165** and **170**. The portraits of Prince Cherkassky and Count Sheremetev, painted by the talented serf artist Ivan Argunov (1727—1802), should be given special mention. Several portraits by the outstanding portrait painters Dmitry Levitsky (1735—1822) and Vladimir Borovikovsky (1757—1825), and the landscapes of Semion Shchedrin (1745—1804) illustrate the flowering of Russian painting in the second half of the eighteenth century.

The water-colours, engravings and sketches in **rooms 164** and **172** acquaint one with Russian architecture. These include in particular items associated with the work of the most outstanding Russian architects of the eighteenth century, Bartolommeo Rastrelli, Vasily Bazhenov (1737—1799), Matvey Kazakov (1738—1812/13) and Ivan Starov.

In **room 169** special attention should be paid to the "egg-shaped" clock designed by the distinguished self-taught Russian mechanic Ivan Kulibin (1735—1818). The small clock, the size of a goose's egg, has more than four hundred parts, which set in motion three mechanisms —one clockwork, one musical, and the third which animates miniature

KULIBIN.
"Egg-shaped" clock

gold figures. Kulibin worked on the clock for more than three years and made it so well that the complex mechanism remains to this day in good working order.

Russian craft industry and folk art are widely represented in **rooms 167**, **173** and **174** by articles made of silver, metal and glass, tapestries, and some wood and ivory carvings. Included in the rich collection of eighteenth century porcelain are some rare examples—a cup, ornamented with a grape design (1749), and a snuff-box (1752) produced at the Imperial Porcelain Works in St Petersburg by the father of home-produced porcelain, Vinogradov (1720—1758).

In **rooms 173** and **174**, among items made by ivory carvers from the town of Kholmogory near Archangel, is an elegant, openwork carved vase,

VINOGRADOV.
Porcelain cup

created by N. Vereshchagin. The chief attraction here is the splendid
collection of articles made in Tula from polished steel—weapons, caskets,
decorative tableware, chessmen—the surfaces of which are adorned with
rose-cut steel "heads".

The Gold Room contains some very rare examples of Russian jewellery dating from the seventeenth to twentieth century.

Russian Culture: 1800—60
Rooms 175—187

The first three rooms contain exhibits which give a general picture
of the social history of Russia in the first quarter of the nineteenth
century. There are portraits of the representatives of the main social
classes of the Russian state, examples of costumes of that period, and
also prints showing towns and villages.

A rare collection of drawings and water-colours illustrates the War of
1812. On the walls are portraits of those who fought in the war. Also of
interest are sets of caricatures by I. Terebenev, I. Ivanov and A. Venetsianov, displayed in the glass cases.

Room 177 reflects the activities of the Decembrists. Only the most significant material is on show, that illustrating the more important stages of the Decembrist movement, which influenced the further development of the revolutionary ideas. V. Timm's picture *14th December 1825* occupies the central place, being one of the few canvases on that subject painted in the nineteenth century.

In this room there is also a beautiful suite of furniture typical of those to be seen in the houses of the rich at the beginning of the century, silk wall panels, bronzes and porcelain.

Room 178 is a library in English style. The walnut furnishings were made in 1894 at the Meltzer Furniture Factory in St Petersburg.

Rooms 179—182 are devoted to the flowering of the arts and sciences in Russia in the first half and middle of the nineteenth century. One's attention is drawn to a bronze bust of Pushkin, cast from I. Vitali's original in 1841−42. This stands out as one of the best sculpture portraits of Pushkin, both by its artistic mastery and by the expressiveness with which the sculptor conveys Pushkin's poetic inspiration.

Portraits of Gogol, Saltykov-Shchedrin, A. Ostrovsky, Goncharov and I. Turgenev witness to the flowering of Russian literature, criticism and theatre. Under the *Portrait of Gogol*, painted in the early 1840s by F. Müller, is displayed a copy of the prose poem *Dead Souls*, published in 1842, and also A. Agin's delightful drawings for that work.

The *Portrait of I. S. Turgenev* is interesting in that it was drawn from life by the German artist K. Lessing during Turgenev's stay at Baden spa in 1876.

Room 183 contains works typical of Russian folk art in the first half of the nineteenth century, with its highly distinctive qualities and centuries-old traditions. One's attention is drawn to a collection of distaffs in a wide variety of shapes and patterns, made by unknown masters from various Russian provinces. The first half of the eighteenth century saw the flowering of many forms of folk art, in particular wood-carving, pottery, weaving, needlework, and decorative lacquerwork.

In **room 184** are displayed architect's drawings, prints, lithographs and paintings which acquaint the viewer with the work of the greatest architects of the first half of the nineteenth century, and with the architectural aspect of Russian towns and cities at that time.

Room 185 contains numerous exhibits which illustrate the great achievements of Russian applied art in the first half of the nineteenth century. These objects have the distinctive simplicity, organic harmony and clarity of line which are characteristic of Russian Classicism. An example of this style is provided by a suite of gilt furniture with upholstery produced at the St Petersburg Tapestry Workshop in 1806. The two tapestries representing Saturn and Aurora also belong to this suite and the ensemble adorned one of the rooms in the Winter Palace.

An important role in interior design was played by bronze: chandeliers, candelabra and vases. Those produced at the Imperial Glass Works were particularly renowned. At the beginning of the nineteenth century the famous architect Rossi became chief designer for that factory—the oldest in the country. The large cut-glass vases, the candelabra and standard lamps in this room were made from his drawings. Articles from the Imperial Glass Works are notable for the rich effect of the faceted glass which harmonizes with the gilded bronze setting.

Some of the finest examples of Russian porcelain are displayed in the cases by the window. Besides articles produced by the Imperial Porcelain Factory, St Petersburg, there are items from the private factories of Gardner, Batenin, Popov, as well as ivory carvings and articles made of tortoise-shell and horn.

Room 186. The paintings, prints and miniatures in this room illustrate the development of Russian artistic life in the first half of the nineteenth century. The distinguished Russian artist of the first half of the nineteenth century Briullov (1799—1852) is represented by the *Portrait of Bobrinskaya*. There are also works by his pupils Kapkov (1816—1854) and Orlov (1812—1863), and by the talented serf artists Tropinin (1776—1857), Argunov (1771—1829) and Tulov. The work of the pupils of Venetsianov is also well represented.

There are also interesting pictures of interiors in the Winter Palace, a rare collection of which is preserved in the Hermitage.

In **room 187** are exhibits illustrating the disintegration of the feudal system in Russia in the middle of the nineteenth century. Water-colours and lithographs by Timm (1810—1895) and Filippov (1830—1878) portray various episodes in the Crimean War of 1853—56, the heroism of the soldiers defending Sevastopol.

Kolyvan vase. Revniukha jasper. 1829—43

The fine portraits by Gay (1831—1894), founder member of the Society for Circulating Art Exhibitions, are a reminder of the awakening of social consciousness in Russia, of the new ideas for the reform of the old system. These portraits depict Herzen and Nekrasov. There is also a portrait of Chernyshevsky (?) by Petrov (1833—1882).

The exhibition ends with a display of material relating to the peasant reform of 1861.

A selection of Russian seventeenth to twentieth century *objets d'art* is displayed in the **Gold Room.**

Russian Semiprecious Stoneware

The Hermitage is rightly called the treasure house of Russian semiprecious stone. Numerous vases, bowls, candelabra and table-tops cut out of semiprecious stones from the Urals and Altai, and now housed in the museum, were created in the nineteenth century in the lapidary works of Peterhof, Kolyvan and Ekaterinburg. Exhibited in **rooms 189, 192, 238** and **241** are various objects made of malachite. In **room 237** stand some magnificent vases of deep blue lapis lazuli mined in Badakhshan. They were produced in the Ekaterinburg workshop, according to the specific method of Russian mosaic, by the gifted craftsman Nalimov (1807—1867), who also executed some floor-lamps made of rhodonite. In **room 249** note especially an elegant vase hewn out of greyish violet porphyry and richly ornamented with bronze. The creator of this vase was Strizhkov (1768—1811) who for many years worked at Kolyvan. In **room 128** (ground floor) stands the Kolyvan vase, named so after the town of its origin. The vase weighs almost nineteen tons and is two hundred and sixty centimetres (8.5 ft.) in height. The vase, cut from a monolith of jasper, took over fourteen years to complete, from 1829 to 1843. During the course of the work the base was divided into several parts, whereas the bowl, five hundred and six centimetres in diameter (almost 16.5 ft.), was made from one block of stone. In spite of its enormous size, the vase is remarkable for its nobility of form and for the perfection of the finish.

THE DEPARTMENT
OF THE PREHISTORIC CULTURE

The department of prehistoric culture was created in 1931 upon the basis of the vast amount of material collected by Soviet archaeologists, supplemented by groups of relics of the past (the Siberian collection, the Scythian antiquities, etc.) preserved in the Hermitage before the October Revolution. Arranged in **rooms 11—33** on the ground floor of the Winter Palace, the exhibition entitled Relics of Prehistoric Culture on the Territory of the Soviet Union provides an excellent means of estimating the successive development of prehistoric society, from the ancient Stone Age up to the Iron Age, from the first appearance of man until the breaking up of the primitive communal system and the formation of states.

Room 11. Palaeolithic and Mesolithic relics, 500,000—7000 B.C. In cases 1 and 2 the most ancient exhibits are displayed: stone implements five hundred thousand to three hundred and fifty thousand years old. They are heavy chisels unearthed by a Soviet archaeological expedition on the Satani-Dar hill in Armenia, oval, triangular and almond-shaped, produced by means of a double-sided whetting of stone by stone. The Satani-Dar chisels, unlike the frequently found flint implements, are made of obsidian.

The first artistic creations appeared during the Palaeolithic Age—statuettes carved out of stone, mammoth ivory and reindeer antlers, and also drawings on the walls of ancient caves. Primitive man depicted various wild animals; another popular subject was the hunt; most important was the theme of the woman as the ancestress of the tribe, and the protectress of hunters.

Twenty female statuettes called the "Venuses of the Stone Age" were discovered during excavations on the site of a hunting camp near the village of Malta in the vicinity of Irkutsk (case 10). These sculptures are between twenty-five and thirty thousand years old. Of approximately the same age is a unique relic of Palaeolithic art, a picture of a mammoth carved on an ivory tablet unearthed at Malta (case 10). Primitive man reproduced the gigantic animal, his most dreaded enemy yet most welcome quarry, with amazing accuracy and vividness. Similar representations were closely connected with magical rites ensuring, according to the native notions of these ancient people, a successful hunt. The nature of Palaeolithic burials—for example the grave of a child whose corpse was sprinkled with red pigment (ochre, symbol of fire and life) and supplied with ornaments and implements of work—affirms the existence in that distant age of notions of life beyond the grave (case 9).

Rooms 12 and 13. Relics of the Neolithic and Bronze Ages of forest regions (5000—500 B.C.) and the steppes in the south of the USSR (3000—700 B.C.). Exhibited in **room 12** are numerous items, discovered during excavation work on the sites of the Neolithic settlements of hunters and fishermen in Karelia, Siberia, the Urals and in the central forest regions, which show that the New Stone Age man made great progress, possessing various methods of working in stone such as boring and grinding, and that he widely used wood and bone (see the stone axes, with wooden and bone handles, sinkers for fishing nets, fishing hooks, arrowheads and wooden fragments of boats, skis and sledges). An important event in the life of Neolithic man was the invention of earthenware, which was decorated with simple designs in the form of hollows and oblique notches.

The Hermitage possesses excellent examples of Neolithic art, among them drawings on stone representing hunting scenes. Discovered on the cliffs of the north (Devil's Nose Cape on the eastern coast of Lake Onega, and the lower reaches of the river Vyg which flows into the White Sea), the drawings came into the museum in 1935. Amongst these impressive designs, drawn on the surface of granite by means of stone tools in the second millennium B.C. (the tribes of the north were not familiar with metal at that time), we can recognize, in spite of the schematized outlines, boats with oarsmen and the figures of animals (elks and deer) and birds (swans and ducks). One genuine masterpiece of Neolithic sculpture is the head of a she-elk, made of horn, found in the province of Sverdlovsk during work in a peat-bog. There are also some stone carvings of fish, from the area of Lake Baikal, used as fishing bait (case 8 and 27).

Room 13. At the time when the tribes of the forest regions were still engaged in hunting and fishing, agriculture was already being practised in the southern parts of the country as early as the Neolithic Age. Ceramics excavated in the village of Tripolye near Kiev are characteristic relics of the so-called Tripolye culture (3000—1000 B.C.), the oldest agrarian culture in the lands now belonging to the Soviet Union. There are some beautifully shaped clay vessels for keeping water, oil and grain, decorated with either intricate carving or a painted design. Some figurines of a female deity and animals, and small models of dwellings are also made of clay (case 11). During the second millennium B.C. the tribes of the south learnt how to obtain bronze and how to cast from it different articles (see the relics from the areas of the Volga, Don and Dnieper rivers in cases 15—17). The Stone Age was superseded by the Bronze Age. It was the working of metal that provided the basis for the first specialized craft, developed by the tribal community in the course of their work. It is interesting to note in connection with this a set of implements used in the production of castings—clay moulds and crucibles for the smelting of metal, and a stone hammer for forging things in bronze (*c.* 1500—1100 B.C.) from the grave of a founder near the village of Rakhinka not far from Volgograd (case 18).

Room 14 contains relics of the Neolithic and Bronze Ages and the early Iron Age in the Caucasus (3000—500 B.C.). A burial mound, dating back to the end of the third millennium B.C. and the beginning of the second and discovered at the end of the last century at Maikop, represents an interesting collection of items from the early Bronze Age in the Caucasus, at that time inhabited by sedentary tribes of cattle-breeders and farmers. This burial mound contained treasure unusually rich for those times.* Together with some polished stone tools and flint arrowheads were found also tools made of copper, a gold vessel and some silver ones with landscapes schematically suggested by a few lines and pictures of animals engraved on them, and ornaments—diadems, beads, bracelets, rings—made of gold, silver, turquoise and cornelian. Four stocky, sharp-horned young bulls, two cast in gold, the other two in silver,

---

* In the Gold Room.

adorned the supports on which hung a canopy erected above the corpse, which was strewn with flame-coloured vermilion (red mercuric sulphide). The cloth of the canopy rotted, and all that remains are some gold rings and small ornamental figured plaques with which the canopy was embroidered. Among the items on view in this room, discovered in Georgia, Armenia, Ossetia and Daghestan, are some of which special mention should be made; these are bronze castings, relics of the so-called Koban culture (named so after the Caucasian village of Upper Koban). Much of the bronze work from Koban consists of axes, fibulae, buckles, bracelets and pins, finely made and adorned with engraved designs.

Rooms 15—21. The art and culture of the Scythian epoch (700—200 B.C.). The collection of Scythian antiquities in the Hermitage is of world renown and provides a vast amount of material for studying the way of life of tribes living on the southern steppes of the European part of the USSR. The collective name "Scythian" is used to describe ethnically heterogeneous tribes speaking a tongue belonging to the Persian family of languages. The burials reflect the social stratification of the Scythian community, which was at the stage when the primitive structure of society breaks up. The ordinary members of the tribe were buried in shallow holes in the ground, and into the grave were put only "the most necessary things" for the "life beyond the grave"—some food in clay vessels, a knife, a few bronze ornaments, and occasionally, in the case of a man, a horse was buried alongside. The graves of the tribal chiefs were large, spacious vaults where, together with the dead person, were buried his wives, servants, horses, expensive weapons, utensils, and objects made of gold and silver. Above the grave was erected a burial mound, in the construction of which the whole tribe took part. The highest of the Scythian tumuli, the Chertomlyk mound on the river Dnieper, reaches a height of twenty metres (over 65 ft.).

Belonging to the very earliest are six large mounds (sixth century B.C.) excavated between 1903 and 1904 in the village of Kelermesskaya in the North Caucasus **(room 15)**. Although these mounds were to some extent plundered in ancient times, they nevertheless afforded material of great value. Among these objects is a large gold plaque* in

---

* The gold objects in the Scythian collection are on display in the Gold Room; shown in the exhibition are some copies produced by galvanoplasty.

Gold comb. Solokha burial mound, 400 – 300 B.C.

the form of a panther which, like the gold stag found in the Kostromskaya burial mound (**room 21**), at one time adorned the shield of a Scythian warrior. The Kelermesskaya panther and the Kostromskaya stag are matchless relics of sixth century Scythian art, characteristic examples of the animal style. The representation of the animal, the only motif in this style, is remarkable for its terseness and wealth of expression, traits of realism interwoven with an original form of stylization. Our acquaintance with early examples of Scythian culture is furthered by a look at some objects found in mounds excavated in the village of Ulsky in the Kuban region, in 1898 and between 1908 and 1910. These mounds are typical of those of the Scythian ruling class, where the dead person was accompanied to the grave by a large number of horses. Thus, in the

Chariot. Pazyryk burial mounds, 500 — 400 B.C.

Rug. Pazyryk burial mounds, 500 – 400 B.C.

largest of those graves in the village of Ulsky, was buried a herd of three hundred and sixty animals.

Room 16 introduces us to the famous fourth century Scythian burial mounds of Solokha and Chertomlyk, situated at the place where, according to the ancient Greek historian Herodotus, who left behind a description of Scythia, the "royal Scythians" lived, having brought into subjection tribes of nomad and ploughmen Scythians. Herodotus informs us that the royal Scythians buried their "kings", i.e. chiefs, in the lands of the Gerrhi which cover approximately the territory of the present-day province of Zaporozhye. The Solokha mound, on the left bank of the Dnieper, not far from the town of Nikopol, was excavated from 1912 to 1913. An embankment eighteen metres high (58.5 ft.) concealed two vaults; one of them, in which was found a woman of high birth, proved to have been plundered—all that remained were two horses in rich attire, gold dress ornaments, a gold needle and two vessels, one silver, the other bronze. The second vault, remarkable for its extraordinary riches, contained the body of a chief, his weapon-bearer, a servant, five horses and a stableman. The head of the dead chief was covered with a heavy bronze helmet; gold rings and bracelets adorned his arms, and around his neck was a gold, crescent-shaped ornament (*grivna*). The splendour of the attire, embroidered with gold plaques, was further heightened by an iron sword in a gold sheath and a delicately wrought gold phial—a symbol of power. Hundreds of bronze arrowheads, seven silver vessels, a ladle and sieve for wine, three enormous pots with remnants of food—this is far from being the complete list of objects found in the grave. Beside the head of the chief lay a comb, the only relic of antique jewellery of its kind. The gold comb from the Solokha mound—12.3 cm (4.7 in.) high and weighing 294.1 grams (10 ounces)—has nineteen tetrahedral teeth, above which runs a frieze formed by the figures of reclining lions. The frieze is surmounted by a sculptural group: a horseman, accompanied by a lightly armed foot-soldier, is repelling the attacks of his enemy who has dismounted as a result of an accident—his wounded horse is fighting in its death throes and blood is pouring from a deep neck wound. The outward appearance of the Scythian warriors, their clothes and their weapons are reproduced with a documental-like accuracy. The Solokha comb, like the majority of the items of luxury from the Scythian burial mounds, is of Greek origin, evidence of the close trade connections between the Scythians and the Greeks.

The colossal Chertomlyk burial mound was excavated from 1862 to 1863. The underground vault contained several chambers, accommodating the graves of a king, a queen and a servant girl, two weapon-bearers, a servant, two stablemen and eleven horses. In the storage chambers were found the remains of woolen dresses which had hung on iron hooks driven into the wall, and on the floor, beside the royal crowns, hundreds of gold plaques which had fallen from the clothes as the cloth had rotted. From the main grave, plundered in ancient times, came swords and a quiver for holding arrows and bow covered with gold leaf, on the surface of which was an embossed multifigured design based upon themes from the ancient myth about Achilles. Harsh retribution befell the thieves; they removed the objects from the ground in parts through a hastily made entrance, and during one such trip a landslide occurred, the rob-

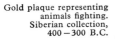

Gold plaque representing
animals fighting.
Siberian collection,
400 — 300 B.C.

bers being buried beneath the fallen earth. Thousands of years later archaeologists discovered the skeletons of two crushed men. In the grave of the queen, untouched by thieves, were found a large number of decorative objects and a famous Greek amphora vase made of silver with the figures of Scythians taming horses in relief **(Gold Room)**.

Rooms 18 and 19. During recent years Soviet archaeologists have made a valuable contribution to science with new information concerning the culture of sedentary tribes of farmers from the Dnieper, Bug and Dniester areas during the period of 700—100 B.C. To defend themselves from the raids of the Scythian nomads, the ploughmen were obliged to fortify their settlements, examples of such fortifications having been found at the sites of Nemirovskoye near the town of Vinnitsa, excavated from 1946 to 1948, and Grigorovskoye in the vicinity of Mogiliov, where excavation work was carried out between 1952 and 1955. Behind the defence ramparts at Nemirovskoye, which reach a height of nine metres (a little over 29 ft.), were found the remains of dwellings, some utensils, various objects made of ivory and bronze, and ceramics of local and Greek origin.

The matchless wealth of the Hermitage collection makes it possible to cast some light, in separate exhibitions, on different aspects of Scythian culture. Thus, in **room 17** are the weapons, clothes and objects pertaining to the rituals and religion of the Scythians; **room 20** provides an introduction to the economic system of those Scythians from the forest steppes; **room 21** is concerned with Scythian art and trade connections with Greece, and also includes relics of Meotae tribal culture, in many respects close to that of the Scythians (the burial-ground at Mozdok, 600—500 B.C., the Karagodeuashkh mound, 400—200 B.C., and the burial-ground near the village of Ust-Labinskaya, 400—200 B.C.).

Rooms 22, 23, 25, 28—32 are devoted to the Altai burial mounds dating from the period 500—200 B.C. Bearing close affinity to the culture of Scythians living near the northern shores of the Black Sea is that of the ancient Altaic peoples, about which much became known as a result of the remarkable discoveries made by the Leningrad archaeologists S. Rudenko and M. Griaznov. Between 1929 and 1949 they excavated five stone mounds (500—300 B.C.) in the high mountain valley of Pazyryk (see **rooms 25, 26** and **28—32**). In a grave beneath one of the mounds was found a timber structure, the "dwelling place" of the deceased. In the coffin, hollowed out from a tree trunk, lay the bodies of a chief and his wife or concubine who, according to custom, was killed after the death of the husband and buried along with him. Outside the timber structure were unearthed the carcasses of horses fully equipped, with bridles and saddles. Thanks to the permafrost which had formed beneath the mounds, the contents of the grave, which were filled with ice, were in an excellent state of preservation; not only the articles made of ivory, wood and metal, but also things which, in normal soil, would in time have disappeared without a trace—corpses, clothes trimmed with sable, squirrel and ermine, equine apparel of hide and felt, musical instruments, and even food. In a small leather pouch was a white mass which, on analysis, turned out to be cheese. Among the most interesting discoveries was an enormous wooden chariot, the different parts of which were fastened together by leather straps, with no metal used at all. During the last year of excavations two remarkable rugs were found. The first of these, made of felt and measuring 6.5 by 4.5 metres (21 by 14.5 ft.), contains an *appliqué* design in coloured felt representing many times over the figures of a goddess seated on a throne and a horseman. The other rug, the only one of its kind, is apparently of Persian origin, four square metres in size (42 sq. ft.) and woven from wool with a soft, velvet-like pile and a beautifully preserved coloured pattern. This rug, the oldest in the world, is almost two and a half thousand years old.

The objects found in the Pazyryk graves were made with great skill, and here, as in the Scythian relics, the animal style is predominant. Stylized representations of animals adorn not only household objects, but are also found in the design of the tattooing which covers the body of one of the chiefs.

For the first time in the history of archaeology ancient objects made of materials very susceptible to decay, for example silk, fur and wood, were unearthed, in such an unusually good state of preservation and in such large numbers that several museum rooms were required to house them all. The rich burial treasures of the ancient Altaic population were also found in the villages of Tuekta (**rooms 22 and 23**) and of Bashadar in the Altai region (**rooms 26, 29 and 30**).

Also related to this group of relics of early nomad art are the ancient gold objects—belt buckles, fibulae, *grivnas* (crescent-shaped neck ornaments) and parts of horses' apparel—of the famous Siberian collection made by Peter the Great (**Gold Room**).

The exhibitions in **rooms 24, 27 and 33** include three large sections —the art and culture of the inhabitants of the southern steppes of the USSR, 300 B.C.—1000 A.D.; the art and culture of the Finno-Ugrians, Balts and Slavs, 700 B.C.—1200 A.D.; and the art and culture of the nomads of the southern steppes, 900—1200 A.D. The items in the exhibition, enormous in number, are interesting not only in themselves but because they also prepare one for the subsequent exhibition entitled The Culture of Old Russia. In the first section the outstanding feature is the collection of relics of Sarmatian culture, the Sarmatians having led a nomadic existence during the fourth century B.C. on the rich pasture lands of the Volga steppes, and later, in the second century B.C., crossed the Don and forced out the Scythian nomads there, occupying a vast area of land stretching as far as the Dniester. The exhibition presents both relics of local origin and others which were imported, reflecting the extensive ties between the Sarmatians and the world of classical antiquity, from which the Sarmatian ruling class obtained decorative objects and finery in return for slaves, cattle, grain, honey, wax and fish. Of great interest are the items from the Khazar fortress of Sarkel, which stood on the banks of the Don where the smooth surface of the artificial Tsimliansk Sea now stretches. Erected in the year 834 A.D., the fortress was captured in 965 by the Russian Prince Sviatoslav, who built on the site Belaya Vezha. Material from the excavations of Belaya Vezha can be seen in the Culture of Old Russia exhibition in **room 145**.

From the ninth to the twelfth century vast areas of land from the Volga to the Don were occupied by tribes of Turkish origin—Pechenegs, Torks and Polovtsy. Displayed in one of the rooms are objects found in burial mounds along the Dnieper, Don and Kuban rivers which give us some idea of the way of life of the nomadic peoples living on the southern Russian steppes.

THE DEPARTMENT
OF THE ART AND CULTURE
OF THE PEOPLES OF THE EAST

Preserved in the Hermitage are more than one hundred and forty thousand items pertaining to the culture and art of the various peoples of the East. This Eastern department was set up in 1920 upon the initiative of the distinguished Soviet scholar and orientalist J. Orbeli.

At the present time the Soviet East is represented in two exhibitions — The Art and Culture of the People of Central Asia: 4000 B.C. — early 20th century and The Art and Culture of the Peoples of the Caucasus: 1100 B.C. — 19th century, situated on the ground floor of the Winter Palace.

The art of the non-Soviet East is presented in the following exhibitions:

Ground floor

The Art and Culture of Egypt: 4000 B.C.-6th century A.D.
The Art and Culture of Babylon, Assyria and Neighbouring Countries: 4000 B.C.-3rd century A.D.

Second floor

The Art and Culture of Byzantium: 5th-15th centuries.
The Art and Culture of the Countries of the Near and Middle East: 3rd-19th centuries.
The Art and Culture of India: 17th-20th centuries.
The Art and Culture of China: 2000 B.C.-20th century.
The Art and Culture of Mongolia: 100 B.C.-19th century.
The Art and Culture of Japan: 17th-20th centuries.
The Art and Culture of Indonesia: 9th-20th centuries.

The Art and Culture of the Peoples of Central Asia:
4000 B.C.—early 20th century
Ground floor, rooms 34—54

The exhibitions present the most important stages in the artistic and historical past of the Tadjik, Uzbek, Turkmen, Kazakh and Kirghiz Soviet Socialist Republics.

Room 34. Central Asia, 4000 B.C.—4th century A.D. During recent years Soviet archaeologists have discovered ancient relics of the culture of farming and cattle-breeding tribes in Central Asia then at the stage of a primitive communal system. These relics include ceramics bearing geometric designs and the stylized representations of animals, anthropomorfic statuettes of clay and stone, and some bronze celts (cabinet 1). In the first millennium B.C. some slave-owning nations lived in Central Asia. One of these was Parthia, and in the centre of the room are displayed some excellent examples of the Parthian art of the second and first centuries B.C. found at the excavation site in the town of Nisa, near present-day Ashkhabad—rhytons made from elephant tusks with a very delicate carved design. Each vessel is horn-shaped and surmounted by the half-figure of a centaur or griffin. Dating back to the time of the ancient Kushan Empire is the celebrated Airtam frieze, a stone relief of the first century A.D. with half-figures of musicians among the rich foliage of an acanthus. One fragment of the frieze, which long ago decorated a temple in northern Bactria near the Uzbek town of Termez, was found quite by accident by frontier guards at the bottom of the Amu-Daria river. The excavations which were carried out after this led to the discovery of other parts of the frieze. The acanthus leaves reveal the influence of antiquity, although the types of face, the hair-styles, clothes, musical instruments and finery—necklaces, earrings and bracelets—testify to the local origin of the relic.

Rooms 35—37. Central Asia, 3rd—8th centuries A.D. These rooms contain unique examples of the monumental decorative art of the Middle Ages, discovered in recent years at Toprak-kala, Pyanjikent and Varakhsh.

The Toprak-kala excavations, on the lands of ancient Khwarezm, unearthed the palace of the third and fourth century rulers of Khwarezm, a fortified three-towered castle with state apartments and living and domestic quarters. The rooms were decorated by tinted clay sculptures and murals painted in mineral pigments on clay plaster previously primed with a thin layer of alabaster. From Toprak-kala there are the statue of a woman, fragments of sculptural groups and a fragment of a wall painting entitled *Woman with a Harp* (**room 35**).

Ancient Pyanjikent, sixty kilometres from Samarkand in the outskirts of modern Pyanjikent, was the capital of the Sogdian principality in the seventh and eighth centuries. Discovered during excavations were two temples, groups of houses belonging to noblemen, country estates and some excellent works of art. Among these is a fragment of a large frieze of unbaked painted clay, which apparently adorned the colonnade of a temple dedicated to the deity of the river Zeravshan. Represented on the frieze are the inhabitants of an underwater kingdom rising from out of the waves—a Triton with the body of a man and a fish's tail, a dragon, a dolphin and several others (**room 35**). Many examples of wooden sculpture were also found at Pyanjikent, the highlight of the collection being the statue of a dancing girl. The Pyanjikent murals produce an indelible impression on the visitor to the museum. Murals in the house of an eminent townsman completely covered the walls of a ceremonial hall, and a fragment of one of them is displayed in **room 37**. It is twelve metres long (a little over 39 ft.), up to 3.6 metres in height (11.7 ft.), and represents scenes of a narrative character—a warrior on a bay horse leaving for a military campaign, another in a duel with a mounted foe, a third fighting a dragon, and suchlike. Fragments from other murals—*The Harper, A Young Man and a Girl on Horses*—further add to one's knowledge of the great artistic skill of the Sogdians, the medieval ancestors of the modern Tadjiks and Uzbeks (**room 35**).

Of great interest is the splendid mural painting in the Hall of the Elephants from the palace of the seventh to eighth century ruler of Varakhsh (near Bukhara), an ancient Sogdian town now buried in sand. This painted frieze depicts a file of men mounted on elephants and the tigers, leopards and griffins that are attacking them (**room 36**). The Varakhsh murals, like those from Pyanjikent, are extremely rare examples of Central Asian monumental art, and were found in a very damaged condition. That the visitor to the Hermitage can admire them on the walls of the museum is to the great credit not only of the archaeologists, but also of the restorers who with tremendous skill and precision and by means of extremely complicated operations, brought back to life these remarkable relics.

In 1932 on the mountain of Mug on the upper reaches of the Zeravshan river, a Tadjik shepherd by chance came across a manuscript written on hide, the first Sogdian document to be found on the territory of Sogdia. In the following year an expedition discovered there the remains of a fortress belonging to prince Divastich, who led the struggle of the Sogdians against the Arabs at the time of the latter's conquest of Central Asia. In the year 722, despite desperate resistance on the part of the Sogdians, the Arabs took their last stronghold, the citadel on Mount Mug. The objects discovered in the citadel are displayed in **room 37** and include local and imported silk and cotton materials, parts of a wooden weaving-loom, a delicately made wicker hair-net, the painted shafts of reed arrows, and utensils. A unique relic from the early eighth century, a fragment of a wooden shield covered with leather and bearing a painted design representing the figure of a Sogdian horseman, is on view in **room 36**, case 3. A great deal is learnt of life in Central Asia during the Middle Ages from written relics **(room 37)**. In a horizontal case near the window is a letter written in Arabic by Divastich to the Arab military leader Al-Djarrakh concerning the fate of the two sons of the Sogdian ruler, who had himself committed suicide. There is also here a small stick bearing an inscription which indicates a path through the mountains. Cabinet 3 contains a large silver vessel with an ancient Turkish inscription: "A present in exchange for the youngest daughter, Giriunchuk, the bride", reminding us of the custom according to which fiancés brought "gifts" to the parents of the bride.

Rooms 38—40. Central Asia, 9th—12th centuries. This exhibition covers almost four centuries, extremely tempestuous in the history of Central Asia. The establishment of Islam after the Arab conquest exercised a pronounced influence upon the nature of art; the realistic representation of man, animals and plants, customary in the art of the pre-Islamic era, gradually gave way to decorative designs, either geometric or stylized floral patterns, with the inclusion of Arabic inscriptions. Similar designs adorned the objects produced by the art crafts which had developed in the towns of Central Asia, prosperous centres of craft industry,

Airtam frieze. Detail. Central Asia, 1st century A.D.

trade and culture in the East during the Middle Ages. Among the specimens displayed in **rooms 38** and **39** are ceramics unearthed during
excavation work on the sites of ancient towns in Central Asia—Paikend,
Afrasiab, Munchak-tepe and Taraz. Exhibited in **room 39** are examples
of ninth to twelfth century bronze, silver and glass ware. **Room 40** is
devoted to architecture, and of particular note are some unglazed carved
tiles which adorned the gates of Samarkand and Uzgent, a manner of
decoration widespread in the Central Asia architecture of the tenth to
twelfth century. Towards the end of the twelfth century glazed tiles
appeared on the scene, one of the earliest examples of which, with a relief
Arabic inscription beneath a turquoise glazing, can be seen in the exhibition (board 4).

Rooms 46 and 47. The Golden Horde, 13th—14th centuries. The
Golden Horde came into existence in the thirteenth century after
Batu-Khan's excursion westwards. It reached the summit of its power in
the fourteenth century during the time of Uzbek-Khan; in the fifteenth
century it split up into separate khanates. A great many of the items in
the exhibition come from the capital of the Golden Horde, Sarai-Berke,
the ruins of which are near Volgograd on the banks of the Akhtuba.
Excavation work was carried out there between 1943 and 1947. **Room 46**
(cabinet 7, case 4) contains items of warrior's equipment and weapons,

which were of great importance in a warlike nation such as the Mongol state (see the helmet, sabres, battle-axe, arrowheads, rings made of bone and used for tightening bowstrings, and the equine apparel).

The numerous objects of art and articles of domestic life were created by craftsmen who had been moved to the Golden Horde capital by force from the conquered lands, including Central Asia, and because of this the Sarai-Berke relics bear a very close resemblance to the relics of Central Asian culture.

The ceramics from Sarai-Berke—glazed pottery **(room 46)** and brightly coloured mosaic tiles for the facing of buildings **(room 47)**—are the work of Central Asian potters, a fact which is evident from the shape of the objects, the decorative designs, the colours, and the way in which they were made. The caravan route from Europe to the East passed through Sarai-Berke, and some fragments of Chinese ceramics, Syrian glassware and a marble candlestick from Egypt are among the items reflecting the trade connections of the Golden Horde **(room 46)**. Of great interest is the silver safe-conduct pass (*paitsza*), which dates back to the fourteenth century and was found in the province of Dnepropetrovsk **(room 47**, case 7). It is a permit for unhampered travel on the territory

Mural from the house of an eminent townsman. Pyanjikent, Central Asia, 7th—8th centuries

A Youth and a Girl on Horses.
Mural. Pyanjikent,
7th—8th centuries

of the Golden Horde, such as was usually given to ambassadors, merchants and foreign travellers.

Rooms 48 and 49. Central Asia, 14th—15th centuries. In the second half of the fourteenth century Central Asia became the centre of the powerful state of Timur (Tamburlaine), and Samarkand the capital of this most formidable conqueror. **Room 48** contains a very unusual historical document, a stone with the inscription in Arabic and Mongolian. The stone, which was found in Kazakhstan, had been placed on the top of a burial mound erected by order of Timur to commemorate his victory over Tokhtamish in 1391. Artists, architects and craftsmen brought from the conquered lands adorned Samarkand. On display in the exhibition are some tiles and carved slabs of marble and limestone—details of the architectural ornamentation of the Bibi-Khanym madrasah, the most beautiful building in Samarkand at that time, erected at Timur's orders between 1399 and 1404 **(room 48)**. There are also some tiles, made in different ways, which embellished the walls of the mausoleums in the famous Samarkand Shah-i Zindeh complex.

In **room 49** there is a wonderful piece of fifteenth century art—the door of the Gur-Emir mausoleum in Samarkand, where Timur and members of his family are buried. The double door, which is made of juniper wood, is covered with the most exquisite carving and bears the remains of silver, copper, nacre, ebony and rosewood incrustation. **Room 48** contains an enormous cast bronze cauldron. It weighs two tons, is one hundred and sixty centimetres high (63 in.) and has a diameter of two hundred and forty-five centimetres (96 in.). The decorative Arabic inscription which encircles the cauldron in three bands states that it is for water, and it was a gift presented by Timur to the mosque of Khwaja Ahmad Yasevi in the present-day town of Turkestan in the Kazakh Soviet Republic. The words "Bless thee" are repeated below ten times; the year in which the cauldron was made, 1399, is indicated, and the craftsman concerned was a certain Abd al-'Aziz from Tabriz. The inscription on the third band is completely taken up by the repeated Moslem dictum "The kingdom belongs to Allah".

Rooms 51—54. Central Asia, late 18th—early 20th centuries. These rooms contain some splendid examples of craft work—famous Central Asian rugs, ceramics from the workshops of Kokand, Khiva, Bukhara and Samarkand, side-arms made by Bukhara and Khiva craftsmen, jewellery, clothes embroidered with gold, and leather goods.

The Art and Culture of the Peoples of the Caucasus: 1100 B.C.—19th century
Ground floor, rooms 55—66

The items displayed in **room 55** confirm the fact that the tribes of Transcaucasia, whose basic occupation was cattle-breeding and to some extent farming, underwent a period (between the eleventh and seventh centuries B.C.) in which the primitive system of communal relations broke up.

Room 56. Urartu, 8th—6th centuries B.C. Urartu, otherwise called the Van empire, the most ancient of the then existing slave-owning nations within what is now the Soviet Union, held a position of supremacy in the first half of the eighth century B.C. among the nations of south-western Asia. The earliest information concerning Urartu was obtained as a result of excavations carried out in 1911 and 1916 by Russian archaeologists on the hill of Toprak-kala, where in ancient times stood the Urartian capital Tushpa (upon the eastern shores of Lake Van in Turkey). Case 1 contains the bronze figurines of winged deities from Toprak-kala, items typical of the Urartian art of the eighth and seventh centuries B.C. The engraved surface of the figurines were covered with gold and coloured with thick paint. The motionless impassive faces made of white stone, with the eyes and eyebrows inlaid with black stone, are nevertheless expressive in their own way. In the past these statuettes, monumental in spite of their small size, embellished the arms of a throne. A very great contribution to the study of Urartian history was made as a result of archaeological excavations at Karmir-blur (Red Hill), from where a large number of the items in the exhibition originate. Many years ago, on Karmir-blur in the environs of Erevan, a fragment of a stone slab was found bearing traces of cuneiform. The inscription gave reason to suppose that at one time a fortress had stood there belonging to the Urartians, an ancient people whose name is preserved in the contemporary name of Mount Ararat. In the summer of 1938 an expedition under the leadership of Academician Boris Piotrovsky began excavations. Upon the strength of the cuneiform inscription found on a bronze door bolt (cabinet 5), the name of the citadel was determined—Teishebaini, i.e. the town of the god of war Teishebas. The research has produced a clear picture of the life and the destruction of Teishebaini, an important administrative and economic centre in the north of Urartu. The fortress received a tribute in the form of foodstuffs, collected from the tribes of Transcaucasia, and after processing this was sent to the capital of the state,

Bronze cauldron. Presented by Timur to the mosque of Khwaja Ahmad Yasevi.
Central Asia, 14th century

Tushpa. Buildings were discovered, intended for the production of
sesame oil, with heaps of oilcake wastage; a workshop for the brewing
of beer, a storeroom for grain, where large quantities of barley, wheat,
millet and flour were kept, and enormous wine cellars with huge vessels
half buried in the earthen floor. It is reckoned that more than four
hundred thousand litres of wine could be kept in these vessels. The
fortress perished around 585 B.C. after a Scythian raid—bronze Scythian
arrowheads were found in the unkilned bricks of the fortress wall.
During the assault a fire broke out, buildings collapsed in the flames,
burying beneath them people and various objects. Much bronzeware was
found in Teishebaini—helmets, shields, quivers and ninety-seven bowls.
These bowls of sparkling golden bronze produce, when struck, a long-
lasting, melodic ring, and in addition each of them, like a bell, had the
sound of a particular key. The inscribed helmet of emperor Sarduris II is

especially noteworthy; the inscription reads: "To the god Khaldis, the protector of Sarduris, from the son of Argistis for his life's sake." Excavations on the fortress are going on, the items found at Teishebaini being sent to the Armenian Historical Museum and to the Hermitage.

Room 58. Transcaucasia, 3rd century B.C.—3rd century A.D. The items displayed here have come from rich burial-grounds discovered upon the lands of Georgia and Armenia at the turn of the century.

Exhibited in a number of cases are objects which have been taken from the burial-ground in the village of Bori near Kutaisi, among them a collection of first and second century bronze vessels of Roman origin and some household articles. A magnificent goblet of ruby-coloured glass with a chased silver rim, dating back to the second century A.D., was found near the ancient Georgian capital of Mtskheta. Glass cases contain some locally made clay vessels and others from Syria, made of glass, which were found in graves near the village of Ashnak in Armenia. A large number of gold objects from the same graves are kept in the Gold Room. Set upon a pedestal is the capital of a pillar from the first century temple at Garni near Erevan, one of the most splendid relics of the architecture of antiquity. A magnificent silver dish (second century A.D.) depicting a Nereid on a sea horse surrounded by Tritons playing in the waves, attracts special attention. The dish is of Roman origin and was found in 1893 near the village of Enkighond in Azerbaijan.

Room 59. Transcaucasia, 4th—8th centuries A.D. Bronze utensils —dishes, censers and pitchers—were brought to the Hermitage in the 1920s from the high mountain village of Kubachi in Daghestan and nearby settlements, where for centuries they had been preserved by local inhabitants. This fine collection of bronzeware occupies an important place among the relics of oriental culture.

Room 60. Northern Caucasus, 1st—10th centuries A.D. The exhibition consists of material from burial-grounds and shrines in Daghestan, Northern Ossetia and the area of the Kuban river. These places were inhabited during the first millennium A.D. by tribes of cattle-breeders and farmers whom ancient writers called Alans. Various discoveries, including

Bronze figure of a deity.
Urartu, 800 — 700 B.C.

coins, confirm that the Alans had connections with Rome, Syria, Parthia, Persia, Byzantium, and the Arab caliphate. From the burial-grounds along the Kuban at the site of Moshchevaya Balka and the village of Khasaut near Kislovodsk comes a unique collection of fabrics. In cabinet 6 are examples of Daghestan bronzeware, statuettes used in rituals and open-work buckles of the seven and ninth centuries. In Northern Ossetia were found some beads made of chalcedony, cornelian and rock crystal, some produced locally, others imported from the northern Black Sea coastlands and from Asia Minor (cabinet 1); silverware (case 3); and Roman glass bottles for incense (cases 2 and 5). In the same burial-grounds in Northern Ossetia were found some Roman enamel fibulae, and belt buckles of local origin (cabinet 14). The outstanding item in the exhibition is a cup (2nd—1st century B.C.) apparently made in Alexandria and found near the town of Mozdok. The cup has two layers of transparent glass, between which is a design in gold leaf (case 2).

Room 62. Medieval Georgia is represented by a limited number of exhibits, among which should be mentioned a collection of chased silver icon frames of the eleventh—twelfth and fifteenth—eighteenth centuries (cases 2, 4 and 13). Special attention may be drawn to some carved details of architectural ornamentation of the sixth to sixteenth centuries.

Room 63. Here there is a much larger collection of items, reflecting the culture of medieval Armenia. From the ancient capital, Dvin, we have some glazed and unglazed ceramics (cabinet 3) and fragments of stucco tiles of the ninth to thirteenth centuries used for decorating interiors (cases 2 and 4). The individual relics originate from the medieval capital of the Armenian kingdom, Ani—for example, fragments of twelfth century frescoes with the representation of the Virgin and Christ, and a stone slab with an inscription in Armenian relating to the erection in 1206 of the Anian fortress gates and towers. Cabinet 13 contains articles found in the fortress of Anberd, excavation work on which was led by J. Orbeli. Special mention should be made of two twelfth and thirteenth century cast bronze mortars, decorated with plant designs, the figures of running animals and a decorative Arabic inscription.

A number of relics are associated with the Kilikian Armenian kingdom, which existed from the twelfth century up to the fourteenth on the north-eastern shores of the Mediterranean. These items include coins of the Kilikian monarch and a silver, three-panel folding icon made in 1293 in one of the Kilikian monasteries (case 17); a beautifully made silver cup, at the bottom of which is depicted the biblical King David playing the psaltery (case 16); and some Armenian illuminated manuscripts (case 14).

The items displayed include locally made ceramics from the site of Oren-kala (twelfth and thirteenth centuries) and others imported from Persia—thirteenth century glazed tiles from the tomb of the Moslem saint Pir Hussein in the village of Khaneka in the Azerbaijanian Soviet Socialist Republic.

Silver dish representing
a Nereid on a hippocampus.
2nd century A.D.

Room 65. Medieval Daghestan. This room contains a rich collection of twelfth and thirteenth century stone reliefs which adorned buildings, no longer preserved, in the village of Kubachi. One of these buildings was apparently the palace of the ruler, another a mosque. The reliefs are remarkable for the variety of subjects; there are scenes from the life of the peoples, a fight between two horsemen, and representations of fantastic animals and birds. Also of interest is a collection of twelfth and thirteenth century Daghestan bronze cauldrons, decorated with the figures of horsemen and beasts and plant designs similar to the depictions of the stone reliefs.

Rooms 61 and **66** contain examples of the work of Caucasian craftsmen from the seventeenth to the nineteenth century which testify to the close bond between their work and national traditions. These items include some woolen rugs, notable for the richness of design and the fine colour harmony. In cabinets 1 and 3 are some glazed ceramic utensils, and case 28 contains a selection of side-arms. Among the objects made of metal can be singled out two cast bronze candlesticks, made in the seventeenth century, with delicately engraved decorative designs. The art of stone and wood carving is represented by some very interesting examples.

The Art and Culture of Egypt:
4000 B.C.—6th century A.D.
Ground floor, rooms 81—91

Room 81. The relics of the ancient period of Egyptian culture in the museum include some Palaeolithic chisels of the fifth millennium B.C., and also earthenware vessels, flint tools and stone palettes for triturating paint dating back to the fourth millennium B.C. (case 1). Belonging to the same period is an interesting group of objects found in 1961 and 1962 by the Nubian archaeological expedition of the Soviet Academy of Sciences at the Khordaud site, one hundred and twenty kilometres south of Aswan (see the vessels, the mortar for pounding grain, palm fruits, the shells of ostrich eggs with geometric patterns, ceramic beads and the ivory bracelet in case 2).

During the period of the Old Kingdom (3000—2400 B.C.) colossal edifices were built, such as the tombs of the Pharaohs—the pyramids—and the tombs of the nobility, upon the walls of which reliefs were carved. One such relief, dating back to between 2500 and 2400, came from the tomb of the high-ranking dignitary Nimaatra. Arranged in rows, the multifigured composition portrays a great nobleman sitting in front of an altar and making an offering. The monumental quality, the immobility and the symmetry, typical of the sculpture of the Old Kingdom, are also clearly evident in a sculptural group made of painted limestone portraying the nobleman Wejankhdjes with his wife Inefertef.

Room 82. The Middle Kingdom (2100—1788) is represented in the exhibition by a number of excellent relics. Note particularly the powerfully impressive statue of black granite representing Pharaoh Amenemhat III which dates from the nineteenth century B.C. The standard immobility of the figure is combined with an expressive rendering of the features and the body muscles. The painted wooden statuettes of servants, oarsmen and ploughmen are remarkable for the great variety of the poses (cases 20 and 22); such *ushabti*-figures were, according to custom, put into the tombs so that even in the life beyond the grave the servants and slaves could carry out the orders of the nobility.

The Egyptians invented a material for writing—papyrus, made from the stems of bulrushes growing in the Nile. In the exhibition there is a world-famous example of Egyptian secular literature, a papyrus dating back to the nineteenth century B.C. entitled *The Tale of the Shipwrecked Sailor*, and also two papyri from the sixteenth century B.C. copied from more ancient manuscripts—*The Instructions of the Pharaoh to His Son Merikare* and *The Prophecy of Neferti*. The first of these contains instructions given to the young emperor concerning the way in which he should govern the nation. The second tells of the rebellion started in Egypt by peasants, craftsmen and slaves about four thousand years ago. A valuable written document from the nineteenth century B.C. has been preserved on the lid of a coffin, in which lay the body of an Egyptian girl; upon the lid is one of the most ancient scripts, the seventeenth chapter of the *Book of the Dead*, a collection of spells for recitation in tombs.

Rooms 83 and 84. The New Empire (1580—1050 B.C.). A bronze dagger blade belonging to Pharaoh Thothmosis III, part of a cuneiform tablet bearing the text of the peace treaty between the Egyptians and the Hittites and a relief portraying an Asiatic man bringing tribute **(room 84)**, all remind us of the frequent wars due to which the New Empire obtained slaves and valuable booty. Several cases contain articles demonstrating aspects of everyday life among the Egyptian nobility—musical instruments, dice, vessels for wine and incense, bronze mirrors, necklaces, bracelets made of faience and glass, metal ornaments inlaid with gold, semiprecious stones and faience, and miniature figures of animals and scarabs carved from stone. An inscription on one of these

Wooden *ushabti*-figures. Egypt, Middle Kingdom

states that Amonhotep III during ten years' rule killed one hundred and two lions while hunting. The monumental sculpture of the New Empire is represented by a statue of the lion-headed goddess Sekhmet (1500—1400 B.C.) from the temple of the goddess Mut at Thebes, and by a sculptural group from the fourteenth century B.C. depicting the chief scribe—the Theban ruler Amenemheb, his wife and mother (granite).

Room 85. In the art of the Last Period (1050—332 B.C.) small bronze sculptures inlaid with gold and silver became very widespread (see, for example, the bronze statuettes in cases 111 and 118).

Rooms 86 and 87. The burial cult of ancient Egypt is illustrated by a number of sarcophagi made of granite and of painted wood, mummies, and the so-called Canopic jars for preserving the viscera of the dead. **Room 87** contains a tablet with funeral prayers for the repose of the deceased's soul, which for a poor man took the place of a sarcophagus. The tablet was attached to the corpse, which was then wrapped in matting and buried in an outlying part of the cemetery. The bodies of Egyptians of high birth were embalmed. For this purpose, as the authors of antiquity tell us, the body, after the brain and internal organs had been removed, was covered with different salts, saturated in balm, wound in a swathing of linen and then laid in the sarcophagus. Displayed in the centre of the room is the mummy of the priest Petese (tenth century B.C.) and three sarcophagi successively inserted into one another. In them lay the mummy just mentioned. It was opened some years ago, at which time many thin linen bandages in a good state of preservation were removed. Also displayed in **room 87** is the swaddled mummy of Babat, the daughter of the priest, and the embalmed mummies of falcons and a cat, regarded as sacred in ancient Egypt.

In the last rooms of the exhibition, which are devoted to the culture of so-called Graeco-Roman Egypt and of the Coptic period, fragments of some Fayum portraits of the second century A.D. deserve particular attention. At the end of the last century some half-plundered tombs were accidentally found by Arabs in the Fayum oasis; instead of the masks customary in Egyptian burial rites, upon the mummy-cases lay portraits painted in encaustic on canvas or on wood, remarkable for their unusual expressiveness. The exhibition concludes with the world-famous collection of the fourth to sixth century Coptic fabrics of linen, wool and silk.

The Art and Culture of Babylon. Assyria and Neighbouring Countries: 4000 B.C.—3rd century A.D.
Ground floor, rooms 92—96

In the very distant past, on the territory of present-day Iraq, there developed, blossomed and finally declined the ancient cultures, successively replacing each other, of states which at one time wielded considerable power—Sumer, Akkadia, Babylon and Assyria. In the valleys of the Tigris and Euphrates at the end of the fourth millennium B.C. and the beginning of the third, an alphabet sprang up—cuneiform—later assimilated by many peoples of the ancient East. In Mesopotamia there was little wood and stone, and so clay, used for building houses and making utensils, was also used for writing on. The cuneiform symbols were

Statue of Pharaon Amonemhat III.
Egypt, 1900 – 1800 B.C.

Coptic fabric representing Gaea, the goddess of the earth. Egypt, 4th century

scratched on a damp tablet with a stick made of bulrush. The exhibition presents cuneiform tablets of different epochs; the earliest go back to the fourth millennium B.C., the most recent to the third century B.C., and they contain extremely valuable historical information. These are documents from temple and imperial archives, depicting the economic system of the slave-owning states of Mesopotamia, legal documents, mathematical, religious and literary texts, exercises in cuneiform calligraphy, and even earthenware "envelopes" used to protect important documents from forgery. In the exhibiton is the world's oldest written relic, estimated to be more than five thousand years old (*c.* 3300 B.C.)—a stone tablet with four symbols of Sumerian ideographic writing in which cuneiform has its origin. Here each symbol expresses an idea or a word.

Among the best examples of Assyrian monumental art are some alabaster reliefs, which bear the remains of the earliest painting. These include examples from the ninth century B.C. with representations of divine guardians and the Assyrian king Ashurnasirpal II, from the palace in the town of Nimrud; some eighth century reliefs depicting priests, from the palace of Sargon II in Khorsabad (Dur-Sharukin), and one

Two warriors.
Relief from a palace in the town
of Nimrud. Assyria,
800 – 700 B.C.

with the figures of an archer and a shield-bearer from the palace of Tig-lath-Pileser III at Nimrud. Reliefs played an important part in the decoration of palace rooms and were an original form in illustrating chronicles, the texts of which were often carved on the walls. These reliefs, specifically intended to glorify the power and might of the cruel Assyrian rulers and to immortalize their victories over enemies, bear the stamp of solemn, austere grandeur. The figures are frozen as it were in solemn poses, and the stony faces, framed in the schematically drawn ringlets of both hair and beard, reiterate the same type again and again.

Depictions of battles and mythological scenes are found in the carving on Assyrian seals and amulets made of semiprecious stones, such as agate, cornelian and chalcedony. The seal, the personal mark of the owner, was used for sealing doors, vessels and large baskets; taking the place of the signature, it ratified orders and treaties. The exhibition also presents Sumerian, Akkadian, Babylonian and Assyrian carved stones, many of which can rank among the finest masterpieces of the craft. In addition the exhibition introduces relics from neighbouring countries: painted vessels from Elam, Luristan bronzeware and Phoenician glass.

Diptych representing circus scenes.
Ivory. Byzantium, *c.* 500 A.D.

The Hermitage possesses a valuable collection of relics from Palmyra. Situated in Syria at the intersection of trade routes, Palmyra served as the intermediary between the countries of the Orient and the Mediterranean coastlands in the second and third centuries A.D. She reached the height of her power in the third century during the reign of Queen Zenobia, when the fame of the beauty of Palmyrian palaces and gardens spread throughout the world. Rivalry with Rome ended with the defeat of Palmyra and her collapse in the year 273. On display is the famous "Palmyrian Tariff", a marble slab with a text in Aramaic and Greek expounding the law issued on April 18th, 137 A.D. concerning the levying of duty on goods imported into Palmyra. The Aramaic part of the text is the most important Semitic stone inscription known to science. Also in this room

St Gregory the Thaumaturgist.
Icon. Byzantium, 12th century

are some second and third century tombstones, —sculptural portraits of the dead carved out of limestone (Khayran, the scribe or a Roman legion, an unknown young woman, and others).

The Art and Culture of Byzantium:
5th—15th centuries
Second floor, rooms 381, 381a, 382

The Byzantine collection in the Hermitage is one of the richest in the world. Its finest part, consisting of silverware, comes from treasures discovered for the most part in the Urals region and in the Ukraine. The

5*

Sassanian silver dish
with the representation
of King Shapur II hunting.
Persia, 4th century

exhibition gives us a clear picture of the peculiar features of Byzantine culture, which developed in the conditions of a growing feudalism, upon the basis of the old traditions of antiquity, and under the influence of ancient oriental culture.

Room 381 is given up entirely to early relics of Byzantine art, some of which were found during excavations in the town of Chersonesus: see the fifth and sixth century relief and marble capitals, and the case containing items of applied art. Special mention ought to be made of two fifth century marble pieces—a representation, traditional in early Christian art, of the Good Shepherd and a bronze polycandelon in the form of a Byzantine basilica.

Room 381a. Antique motifs characteristic of early Byzantine art are found on some sixth and seventh century silver utensils, for example, a dish with the figures of the mythological characters, Meleager and

Faience bottle. Persia, 17th century

Atalanta, and a ewer decorated with figures of sea-nymphs (cabinet 3, case 4). Utensils bearing representations of a cross or a Chi-Rho monogram (cabinet 6), testify to the appearance in art of new tendencies connected with the spread of Christianity. Occupying a prominent place in the exhibition are some items made of ivory, in the working of which Byzantine craftsmen reached a high degree of perfection. One of the outstanding exhibits in the collection is a diptych (*c.* 500) representing circus scenes, in which the tense moments of the contest between man and beast are convincingly conveyed (cabinet 3). The mosaic painting *Angel* is a characteristic example of Byzantine monumental art, specimens of which have been preserved in only a very few cases.

Room 382 contains some interesting tenth to twelfth century caskets embellished with carved ivories depicting venators, actors and musicians. Of exceptional value are some twelfth to fourteenth century icons, including *St Gregory the Thaumaturgist*, *The Transfiguration* (a painting), *St Theodore Slaying the Dragon* (*champlevé* and *cloisonné* enamel), and *Four Saints* (miniature mosaic). Articles made of bronze, glass and wood, fabrics, ceramics, gems, coins and medals all lend the Byzantine exhibition great diversity.

Lamp made of rock crystal. Egypt, 10th century

Bronze vessel in the form of an eagle.
Persia, 8th—9th centuries

The Art and Culture of the Countries
of the Near and Middle East:
3rd—19th centuries
Second floor, rooms 383—397

Rooms 383—391 and 294. Persia, 3rd—18th centuries. The Hermitage boasts the world's largest collection of Sassanian silver. The majority of the Sassanian silverware—jugs and cups for wine, vases and salvers for sweetmeats and fruit—were found by chance in the Urals region and near the river Kama, a tributary of the Volga, to where they had been taken by traders in return for furs. Thus, for example, among the highlights of the Hermitage collection is a dish depicting King Shapur II hunting, found in 1927 in the province of Kirov. Sassanian utensils were generally decorated with relief representations of royal hunting scenes, magnificent feasts, dances, and with the characters from ancient Persian mythology. An example of this is the famous dish upon which is

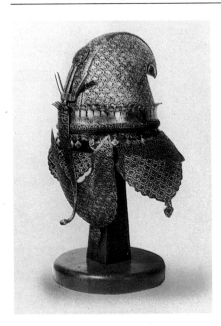

Open-work gilded iron helmet.
India, late 17th century

represented a well-known episode from Firdousi's poem *Shahnameh* describing how Azadeh, the beloved of Prince Bahram-Gur, demanded upon seeing a herd of gazelles that with the help of arrows the prince turn a buck into a doe and a doe into a buck. With a special crescent-headed arrow the prince shot off a buck's antlers, thus turning him into a doe; then he shot a doe, planting two arrows in the place where antlers grow, thus turning her into a buck. In the hunting scenes the faces, costumes and head-dresses of the Persian kings are reproduced with absolute accuracy, and this makes it possible to establish their names. The amazing ability to make the decorative compositions harmonize with the actual shape of the object, the clarity of design and the exquisite execution of detail account for the noble beauty of the Sassanian articles.

Also displayed in this room is a very large collection of Persian carved stones and coins.

Faience dish.
Turkey, 16th century

Room 384. In Persia the manufacture of bronze goods was widely developed. Varied in their shapes and their functions, they were produced by casting and chasing, with subsequent red copper and silver incrustation. Excellent examples of this sort of work are a twelfth century censer in the form of a cat, an aquamanile (1206) representing a female zebu with a calf, and two twelfth century bronze pots made by craftsmen from the town of Gerat.

Rooms 385—387. Persian ceramics, 12th—15th centuries. In the East lustre ware from the northern Persian towns of Kashan and Rayy was very highly esteemed, and there are in the exhibition examples of the work produced in these towns—glazed tiles for facing secular and devotional buildings. These include tiles dating from the thirteenth century which decorated the Imam-zadeh Yakhyya mausoleum in the town of Veramin, and a lustre *mihrab*, a prayer-niche facing Mecca in the wall of a mosque or mausoleum, from Kashan (1305). The most splendid item made by the Kashan craftsmen is a large lustre vase of the thirteenth

JAMINI ROY.
Toilet. India, 20th century

century with the figures, in relief, of musicians, animals and scenes from a game of polo (**room 387**).

In **rooms 391—394** there is a very rich collection of objects produced by craftsmen of the sixteenth to eighteenth century; among these are velvet and silk fabrics embroidered with gold and silver, carpets, copper and bronze utensils, in many cases with the texts of poems by famous Persian poets, ceramics from the towns of Kashan, Isfahan, Kerman and Yezd, damask sabres and daggers adorned with gold inlay and incrustation, lacquers and articles made of coloured glass.

The items displayed in **room 394** reflect the extensive trade connections which Persia maintained with Russia and many European nations. In **room 392** are some miniatures of the Tabriz, Shiraz and Isfahan schools; there are also some originals of the well-known seventeenth century Persian artist Reza-i-Abbasi.

Room 388. Syria and Iraq, 13th—15th centuries. Syria was famous for its glassware with coloured enamel patterns, exported to many distant places, and of interest in this respect is a thirteenth century glass vessel in the form of a horn bearing Arabic inscriptions and the representations of Christian saints. The sixteenth century German-made silver mount was executed, as the inscription says, upon the order of a knight of the Livonian Order, Bruno Drollshagen. Enjoying wide renown were the bronze utensils produced by Syrian and Iraqi craftsmen who, by skilfully applying in their ornamentation engraving, niello and incrustation, could turn simple articles of everyday use into splendid works of art (see, for example, the basins, dishes, candlesticks, etc.).

Rooms 389 and 390. Egypt, 7th—15th centuries. This exhibition provides an introduction to the craft work of Mohammedan Egypt. Notice especially a large collection of seventh to twelfth century fabrics, two magnificent vessels made of rock crystal, some bronzes, glassware and ceramics. The fourteenth century glass lamps **(room 390)** painted with coloured enamels, and with the heraldic emblems and the names of the rulers of the Mameluke dynasty, remind us of Syrian glassware. It is known that after the conquest of the country by the Mamelukes, Syrian glass-blowers were taken to Egypt. Some details of thirteenth to fifteenth century architectural ornamentation are very striking—carved wooden panels for interior decoration, inlaid with ivory and valuable kinds of wood, and bearing a typical geometric design.

Rooms 395—397. Turkey, 15th—18th centuries. As a result of conquests the Ottoman Sultanate became, in the fifteenth century, one of the world's most powerful states. In the centre of one of the rooms is exhibited a remarkable suit of armour belonging to a Turkish cavalry soldier of the fifteenth century. In cabinet 2 is the head-dress of a Janissary, the Janissaries constituting a special corps of the Turkish regular army in the fifteenth and sixteenth centuries.

The collection of Turkish applied art is exceptionally rich. **Rooms 395** and **396** contain sixteenth and seventeenth century ceramics from the towns of Iznik in Asia Minor and Damascus in Syria, prominent centres of the ceramic industry. Eighteenth and early nineteenth century ceramics from the town of Kütahya are displayed in **room 397**. The towns of Bursa, Damascus and Scutari were renowned for their brocade, velvets and silk fabrics (see **rooms 395—397**). Carpets were manufactured everywhere, in Kula, Bergama, Ladik and Chiordes; the finest of the carpets in the Hermitage was made in the town of Usak (**room 396**, frame 15). The favourite decorative motif, adorning ceramics, fabrics and carpets alike, is the representation of flowers—carnations, tulips, hyacinths, wild roses—and of pomegranates. In **rooms 396** and **397** there is an enormous collection of richly ornamented weapons made by craftsmen in Istanbul, Trebizond and Erzurum.

The Art and Culture of India: 17th—20th centuries
Second floor, rooms 368—371

The Hermitage has a rather small, but nevertheless interesting collection of works of both old and contemporary Indian art. The collection in the first section illustrates just one of the stages in the centuries-old history of India—the period of the feudal Mogul Empire from the sixteenth up to the nineteenth century. In the section devoted to contemporary art there are works by the outstanding artists of the present day which have entered the Hermitage in recent years.

The items in **room 368** acquaint the visitor with the art of various regions of the country—Bengal, Southern and Central India, Gujerat, the Punjab. Among these can be seen some small marble, wooden and bronze sculptures of the sixteenth to nineteenth century, more often than not representing the Hindu gods and the heroes of the old Indian epics, *Mahabharata* and *Ramayana*.

From the exhibition in **rooms 369** and **370** special mention should be made of the large collection of seventeenth to eighteenth century miniatures, including examples of the art of the Mogul, Rajputa and small local schools.

Occupying an important place in the exhibition is one of the world's finest collections of old Indian weapons. The offensive and defensive weapons are extremely varied and include helmets of open-work gilded steel, shields made from rhinoceros hide, *pata* swords with an armoured covering protecting the warrior's arm, and *kuttar* daggers with the handle at right angles to the blade. Also displayed are some *chakra*, ring-like

Bodhisattva and monk from the monastery known as the "Cave of a Thousand Buddhas".
9th century
Moon deity. Khara-Khoto, 12th – 13th centuries

missiles with edges as sharp as blades, and side-arms with blades of damask steel (the home of which was India) richly decorated with engraving and incrustation and inlaid with gold and silver leaf. Craft work of the seventeenth to nineteenth century is represented by some wonderful specimens of silk and velvet fabrics, carpets, ceramics, bronzes and objects made from ebony and ivory (**rooms 369** and **370**).

Room 371 contains a collection of modern painting, in which we can note in particular the *Fire Ordeal of Sita* (water-colour on silk) by the famous painter Barad Ukil, *The Road to Mayavahti* by Nandalal Bos, *Shacks and Sands* by Bimal Das Gupta, *A Meeting of Yogis* and *Spring* by S. Roerich, *Returning Home* by Madhava Satvalekar, *Toilet* by Jamini

Roy, and a bust of Mahatma Gandhi by the well-known sculptor Chintamani Kar. There is also a nineteenth century screen of exquisite openwork ivory presented to the Hermitage by Jawaharlal Nehru.

The Art and Culture of China:
2000 B.C.—20th century
Second floor, rooms 351—364

In the first room, from among the material reflecting the culture of ancient China, we should note particularly some very ancient relics of Chinese writing—inscriptions dating from the fourteenth century B.C. on the bones of animals. These texts which were used for telling the future are simple in content — "isn't it time the harvest was begun", "will the hunt be successful" — and they enable us to determine the economic structure of the very ancient inhabitants of the country.

The basis of the exhibition in **room 351** is a rare collection of loess sculpture and some fragments of sixth to ninth century murals, brought in 1914—15 from the monastery of Chi'ien-fo-tung (the "Cave of a Thousand Buddhas") near the town of Tunhuang by the expedition of Academician Oldenburg. Among these relics of medieval art the figures of two monks, a Bodhisattva, and fantastic beasts which guarded the entrance to a temple are particularly striking.

Presented in **room 352** are items found in Khara-Khoto, a dead town discovered among the sands of the Gobi by the Russian traveller Kozlov. At one time this was the capital of the Tangut kingdom, which fell in the thirteenth century under the attacks of Jenghiz-Khan. The paper money, fabrics, ceramics, tools and household articles found at Khara-Khoto testify to the extent to which crafts and trade had developed in this medieval eastern town. Some valuable works of art have come from Khara-Khoto, including paintings on canvas, paper and silk of the Tibeto-Tangutan and Chinese schools, sculptures, and some carved wooden boards for printing books and etchings.

Rooms 354—362 contain porcelains, lacquers, enamels, ivories and examples of painting and sculpture from the period of 1300 to 1900. The exhibition is rounded off by some pieces of twentieth century art;

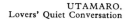

UTAMARO.
Lovers' Quiet Conversation

room 363 contains the work of the famous Chinese artists Chi'i Pai-shih (1872—1957) and Hsü Pei-hung (1894—1953), and in **room 364** there are examples of modern applied art.

The Art and Culture of Mongolia: 100 B.C.—19th century
Second floor, rooms 365—367

The first room **(367)** presents the celebrated group of relics, comprising clothes, fabrics and household objects, from the tumuli of Noin-Ula in the northern part of Mongolia, investigated by Kozlov. The tumuli were the burial place of Hun chiefs, the Huns having formed at the end of the third century B.C. a vast nomadic empire, which included the lands of Mongolia, western China, and part of Central Asia. The Hun tumuli at Noin-Ula date from the beginning of the Christian era. **Room 366** is devoted entirely to items belonging to the time of Jenghiz-Khan's empire; what attracts most interest here is the "Jenghiz Stone", a very ancient relic of Mongolian writing. It is a granite stele with a text and was erected in 1225 at the order of Jenghiz in honour of his nephew Isunke. Of further interest are some architectural details—stone dragon statues and roof from a thirteenth—fourteenth century palace belonging to a relative of Jenghiz-Khan. The ruins of the palace, situated five kilometres from the village of Konduy in the province of Chita, were excavated in 1957 by a joint expedition of scholars from the USSR and the Mongolian People's Republic. In the third room **(365)** there are examples of the Mongolian art of the sixteenth to nineteenth century—painting, sculpture and craft work.

The Art and Culture of Japan:
17th—20th centuries
Second floor, rooms 375 and 376

A prominent place in the exhibition is occupied by woodcuts, one of the most popular forms of Japanese art. In the second half of the seventeenth century a school known as Ukiyo-e ("Pictures of Our Transitory World") developed in the Japanese capital Yedo, present-day Tokyo. The artists of this school, breaking with the traditions of medieval painting which was limited to a number of religious subjects and conventional landscapes, turned to the graphic arts as a more popular form, depicting in their works the life of the townspeople and vivid scenes from their native countryside. Well represented in the exhibition is the work of the most prominent exponents of colour-printing, Suzuki Harunobu (1725—1770), Kitagawa Utamaro (1753—1806), Katsushika Hokusai (1760—1849) and Ando Hiroshige (1794—1858). Japanese engraving, with its variety of subjects, expressiveness of line, beauty of colour and originality of compositional design, became known in the West in the mid-nineteenth century and exercised a definite influence upon the work of many European artists. The exhibition includes the earliest of the

HIROSHIGE. Winter in the Park

thirteenth and early fourteenth century Japanese Buddhist paintings in the Soviet Union with the representation of Kokudzu, a deity giving wisdom and prosperity. The fundamental methods of monochrome painting in Indian ink on silk were brought to Japan from China, and it was in this manner that Tanyu Kano, a well-known artist of the early seventeenth century, produced his album of miniatures (horizontal case by the window).

The Hermitage possesses valuable examples of Japanese decorative and applied art, one of the distinctive features of which is the variety of materials and methods of execution. Miniature statuettes and decorative waist-pendants (*netsuke*), made from bone and wood, depict scenes from the life of the people and from Japanese history, legend and mythology. Also of note are the details on the handles of swords (*tsuba*) made from iron, silver, bronze and different non-ferrous alloys and embellished with incisions and engraving. Refined taste, skill, and a wealth of imagination of the craftsmen are also evident in the lacquers; black and gold Japanese lacquer was particularly famous—see the caskets, and the boxes for Indian ink and brushes, for medicine, tea and tobacco. There are two caskets bearing the signature of the well-known craftsman Ogata Korin (1658—1716).

In the second room there is a fine collection of modern decorative and applied art—articles of clay, lacquer, metal, wood and bamboo, handmade by the foremost Japanese craftsmen. These items include a vase made of forged silver with fish designs; a cotton fabric screen, *Pine Forest*; a forged-iron statuette, *Sea-lion*, and a flame-red lacquer vase. Folk art is represented by ceramic plates and dishes, fabrics, lacquers and wooden toys.

The Art and Culture of Indonesia: 9th—20th centuries
Second floor, room 358

Art and culture of Indonesia is illustrated by specimens from Central Java (ninth—eleventh centuries), Eastern Java (fourteenth—sixteenth centuries) and Bali Island (eighteenth—nineteenth centuries). The collection comprises sculptural pieces—statues of Shiva, Vishnu, Gameshi, etc., objects of cult practices—ceremonial masks and vessels, bronze and wooden objects of artistic crafts, manuscripts, specimens of artistically coloured fabrics (*batic*) and examples of the Javanese national weapon (*kris*).

THE DEPARTMENT OF THE ART
AND CULTURE OF ANTIQUITY

The relics in the Hermitage of the culture of classical antiquity include a very rich collection of vases, carved stones, jewellery and terracotta, a rare collection of Roman portrait busts, and examples of Greek sculpture. The latter is represented in the Hermitage, as in the majority of museums in the world, primarily by first—third century Roman copies from Greek originals, most of which were lost even in antiquity.

The following exhibitions are open to view:

The Art and Culture of Ancient Greece: 800-200 B.C.

The Art and Crlture of Ancient Towns of the Northern Black Sea Coastlands: 700 B.C.-3rd century A.D.

The Art and Culture of Ancient Italy and Rome: 700 B.C.-4th century A.D.

The Art and Culture of Ancient
Greece: 800—200 B.C.
Ground floor, rooms 108, 109, 111—114, and 121

Room 111. The art of the archaic and early classical periods, 800—450 B.C. The oldest examples of Greek art in the exhibition are some ninth and eighth century clay vessels with geometric patterns painted in black or reddish brown pigment (case 1). This ornamental pattern, consisting of circular bands, sometimes includes geometric representations of animals, birds and man. The vessels of the geometric style, like the primitive statuettes of bronze and clay, belong to the era of the tribal system and the birth of the slave-owning city-states, the so-called *poleis*.

Vessel made by the craftsman
Charin from Greece. *C.* 500 B.C.

During the seventh and sixth centuries can be observed the rapid growth of the Greek *poleis* of Miletus, Clasomenus (Asia Minor), Rhodes, Chios, Samos, Athens, Corinth, etc. Busy trade connections were established between them, and trade was likewise developed with the countries of the East. Among the crafts, pottery was the most important. The Corinthian vases of the "carpet" style, the decorative patterns of which bring to mind an eastern fabric, were famous throughout the Mediterranean in the seventh and sixth centuries B.C. (cabinet 2). In Athens, one of the most prominent centres of Greek crafts, trade and culture, the so-called black-figure style was prevalent in the sixth century. Upon the orange-coloured surface of the clay vessel a black silhouette was drawn, and the details were scratched in with a chisel and painted in purple and white pigment.

"Vase with a Swallow". Greece, late 6th century B.C.

These black-figure vessels are extremely decorative, and the shining black pigment, often called lacquer, stands out boldly against the colour of natural clay beneath a transparent glaze (cabinets 7 and 8). Towards the end of the sixth century B.C. and the beginning of the fifth, the black-figure style was replaced by the red-figure style. Now the ground was covered with lustrous black pigment, and the figures were composed in the natural terracotta tones of the clay, all the details painted by brush or quill. This method made it possible to render more vividly and convincingly the multifigured compositions of mythological, epic and genre scenes which usually adorn the surface of Attic vessels. Some vases have preserved the names of their creators; a wine bowl bears the inscriptions "Made by Hischylus" and "Painted by Epictetus". Upon a psykter, decorated with the figures of hetaerae reclining on couches, there is the inscription "Painted by Euphronios". The Hermitage example is one of a group of vessels that have been preserved bearing the signature of this celebrated Greek craftsman of the late sixth and early fifth centuries B.C. Also attributed to Euphronios is the famous "Vase with a Swallow" (case 12). On one vase there is the curious inscription, "Painted by Euphimides, son of Polios, like Euphronios could never do!"

Greek ceramics are extremely varied in shape; there are amphoras —tall vessels with two handles for storing or carrying wine and oil; squat, three-handled hydrias for water; kraters for mixing wine with water; drinking cups—kylices, kanthari and scyphi; and vessels used for storing fragrant oil—narrow-necked lecythi, globe-shaped aryballi, and slender alabastra. Ancient Greek ceramics were famous far beyond the frontiers of Greece and were widely exported.

The small-size bronze sculpture of the sixth and early fifth centuries, B.C., including statuettes of youths and a stand for a mirror in the form of the goddess Aphrodite, introduces us to the archaic style in sculpture. The figures are static and are portrayed full face, with characteristically prominent eyes, and the hair and the folds in the clothes are represented schematically (cabinet 3, cases 5 and 9).

The statue of Hyacinth, attributed to Pythagoras of Rhegium, is evidence of the realist features of Greek art in the first half of the fifth century B.C. The famous sculptor gave the lean, supple body of the youth spatial life. Hyacinth is portrayed watching the flight of the discus.

Temple pendant with the head of Athena. Greece, late 4th century B.C.

Room devoted to Greek art. (400 – 300 B.C.)

Room 112. The art of the Golden Age (500—400 B.C.) The basic theme of the classical period is the portrayal of the athlete, the *victor ludorum*, the bold, valiant defender of his native town, as well as the representation of the gods who personified the wealth and power of the state. The most eminent Greek sculptors during the Golden Age were Myron, Polycletus, and Phidias. Myron, who worked in bronze and whose work survived only in Roman copies, was the creator of the famous statue *Discobolus*. Similar in style to the works of Myron are the statues of a woman (No. 95), of the god of healing Aesculapius (No. 94), and also the head of a fist-fighter (No. 143) displayed in **room 113**.

The basalt head of a youth (No. 140) with a classically regular, tranquil face belongs to the sculpture of Polycletus' circle. It re-creates the celebrated *Doryphoros* (*The Spear-bearer*) executed by Polycletus in strict conformity with his *Canon*, a tractate on the proportions of the human body. Polycletus, like Myron, worked in bronze, but his originals have not been preserved. Other works of the same circle are the torso of an athlete (No. 104a) and the statue of Hermes (No. 104).

The Roman copy of a fifth century marble statue of Athene gives us some idea of Phidias' style; the warrior goddess is portrayed in a calm, majestic pose, leaning against a spear, her head is crowned with a helmet, and the dress, descending in a series of folds, emphasizes the magnitude of the frontally portrayed figure (No. 98). This representation personified the unshakable power of the Athenian state. Two stelae, the tombstones of Philostrata and Theodotus (Greek originals), give us some idea of the classical relief at the time of Phidias.

Room 114. Greek art, 400—300 B.C. The complex social and political situation in Greece during the fourth century B.C. brought about the development in art of several trends, of which Scopas, Praxiteles and Lysippus are good representatives. These great sculptors, differing enormously in their creative individuality, are united by their interest in man's inner world; their portraits of the gods are even more "human" than was the case in the fifth century B.C. Several sculptures in the exhibition are from the school of Scopas (his work has survived only in Roman copies); one of these is the statue of Heracles (No. 272). The hero's muscular body appears tired, and the deeply sunken eyes and the mouth half open in suffering lend a mournful expression to his face. The

Heracles Slaying the Lion of Nemea. 1st—2nd century Roman copy of Lysippus' original
The Resting Satyr. 1st—2nd century Roman copy of Praxiteles' original

fervour of passions—suffering, ecstasy, fury—is the basic theme of
Scopas' work.

His contemporary, Praxiteles, worked mainly in marble. Praxiteles'
heroes are usually portrayed in some light reverie, and in poses full of
indolent grace. The smoothly outlined figures are notable for their
proportions, elongated in comparison with Polycletus' *Canon.* Acquainting the visitor with the work of the great sculptor is a whole series of
items: *The Resting Satyr,* a copy of one of the sculptures by Praxiteles
most popular in antiquity; the head of Aphrodite (No. 300), similar to the
type of the celebrated Aphrodite of Cnidus; *Satyr Pouring Wine,* a copy

of one of Praxiteles' early works, and others. The portrait of the Greek dramatist Menander was executed by Praxiteles' sons, Cephisodotus and Timarchus.

The small marble group called *Heracles Slaying the Lion of Nemea* is a reduced-size copy of a bronze sculpture by Lysippus from a series devoted to the twelve labours of Heracles. The powerful figure of Heracles and the body of the beast are represented in such a way that the group can be viewed from all angles. The sculptor depicts the climax of the duel between man and beast; Heracles is strangling the lion, which, as its strength is sapped, sinks down onto its hind paws. The extent of Lysippus' creative scope can be seen from his *Eros Stringing the Bow* and the statuette *The Feasting Heracles*. He also worked in the field of portraiture, and the head of the great Greek philosopher Socrates was based upon Lysippus' original. His work crowned the achievements of Greek art of the fifth and fourth centuries B.C.

Room 121. The Hellenistic period. Nowadays we have only isolated examples of original works of Greek marble sculpture, whereas much terracotta has been preserved. Elegant terracotta statuettes were made in many cities in Greece, Asia Minor and the northern Black Sea coastlands, though particularly highly esteemed were the items produced in the Greek town of Tanagra, whose craftsmen were influenced by the work of Praxiteles. The Hermitage collection of Tanagra terracottas of the fourth and third centuries B.C. ranks among the finest in the world (cases 3—6). The figurines of girls, youths and children in the costume of that time provide interesting material for studying the Greek way of life. Frequently terracottas reproduce in miniature famous statues of antiquity which have not come down to the present day.

In almost all the rooms of the department devoted to the art of antiquity there are displays of gems—carved stones, which were no less prevalent in the world of antiquity than in the countries of the ancient East. Carving on precious and semiprecious stone was done by hand and on the lathe, which was known in Greece as early as the sixth century B.C. The Hermitage collection includes hundreds of specimens of beautiful intaglios and cameos. The former were known in the Hellenistic period among the aristocracy, who surrounded themselves with luxury previously unheard of. Cameos were inserted into diadems, fibulae and rings, they were used to embellish valuable vessels, or simply preserved as works of art. In one of the horizontal cases by the window is the Gonzaga Cameo, exceptionally beautiful and among the largest of its kind (15.7×11.8 cm—6.14×4.65 in.). On a three-layered sardonyx, almost transparent and fancifully coloured by nature, two exquisite profiles were carved in high relief,—the Egyptian pharaoh Ptolemy Philadelphus and his wife Arsinoë. The Gonzaga Cameo was made in the third century B.C. in Alexandria, the capital of Ptolemaic Egypt and one of the leading centres of Hellenistic culture. The Alexandrian school, in which genre themes in particular were widely developed, frequently treated with naturalistic details, is represented in the exhibition by some characteristic examples: *The Satyr with a Splinter* and *Shepherd with a Lamb*. Such marbles were traditionally placed in the corners of gardens. In this room should be noticed three items representing the school of Pergamum which was influenced by Scopas: the heads of a dying Gaul (No. 501), of a dying giant (No. 21a) and of the dead Patroclus (No. 75), and also moulded copies of the sculptural frieze from the Altar of Pergamum **(room 105)**. From the Rhodes school is the fragment of a statue,—the head of a dying companion of Odysseus (No. 86).

Rooms 108 and 109. Graeco-Roman decorative sculpture. The architecture of **room 108**, completed between 1842 and 1851 by the architect Yefimov according to Leo Klentze's design, reproduced the inner courtyard of a grandiose Hellenistic or Roman house.

The fountain with the statue of Aura, the goddess of the air and the gentle breeze, and some examples of small decorative sculpture—*Eros Holding a Shell*, *The Infant Heracles Strangling the Snakes* and *Boy with a Bird*—at one time adorned similar courtyards and rooms in ancient houses. The realistic portrayal of the child was one of the most significant achievements of the art of the Hellenistic period.

Room 109 contains a wonderful collection of marbles which decorated palaces, villas, gardens and parks during Hellenistic and Roman times; these include statues of Dionysus, Aphrodite, dancing satyrs, and figures of the Muses. Of wide renown is the statue of Aphrodite, later called the Venus of Tauris after the Tauride (Tavrichesky) Palace in St Petersburg, where it was kept from the end of the eighteenth century until the mid-nineteenth. An unknown sculptor of the third century

The Gonzaga Cameo. 300 — 200 B.C.

B.C., inspired by the conception of the Aphrodite of Cnidus, portrayed the beautiful goddess nude; her well-proportioned body is more fragile, her beauty more refined than that of Praxiteles' goddess. The Venus of Tauris, ceded to Peter by Pope Clement XI after protracted diplomatic negotiations, was, in 1720, the first antique statue to appear in Russia.

The Art and Culture of Ancient Towns on the Northern Black Sea Coastlands: 700 B.C.—3rd century A.D.
Ground floor, rooms 100, 115—117, 119 and 120

In 1830 soldiers digging stone on the steppe near Kerch by chance came across, beneath the Kul-Oba burial mound (Tartar, "Hill of Ashes"), a grave dating from the fourth century B.C. containing many valuable objects, among them a large number of gold articles of Greek origin. Underneath the mound in a stone vault three persons were buried, —a warrior of the aristocracy, possibly a Bosporan ruler, his wife and a slave weapon-bearer. A gold vase with the figures of Scythian warriors making camp on the steppe, a crescent-shaped neck ornament (*grivna*) embellished with small figures of Scythian horsemen, a gold phial, weapons ornamented with gold, earrings, pendants, bracelets, plaques—all these were brought into the Hermitage and are kept in the **Gold Room** as part of the unique collection of ancient Greek jewellery. The remainder are in **room 116**, case 22.

The Bosporan kingdom, with its capital at Panticapaeum on the site of present-day Kerch (see **rooms 115, 116** and the case entitled "Panticapaean Necropolis"), lay on both sides of the straits of Kerch—Bosporus Cimmerius. The population of this slave-owning state was made up of Greeks, who had founded colonies on the Black Sea coast as early as the sixth century B.C., and local tribes. The relics found on the territory of the Bosporan kingdom reflect the unusual mode of life which had developed there as a result of the interaction of local and Greek culture. The local tribes dwelt mainly on the steppes, maintaining close contact with the Greek inhabitants of the Bosporan towns. Significant in this respect are the fifth century tombs of the local "hellenized" ruling class from the "Seven Brothers" burial mounds near the Kuban (**room 116**, case 12). The graves, in which according to local custom horses were buried along with the deceased, yielded many objects of Greek origin. Of an obviously Greek character is the grave of a woman discovered at the end of the last century on the Taman peninsula near ancient Phanagoria (**room 115**, case 16). Here, among other things, were unearthed some famous fancy-shaped vessels for keeping fragrant oil made by Greek craftsmen at the end of the fifth century B.C. The finest of these, in the form of a sphinx— a fabulous creature with the face of a woman, the body of a lion and the wings of a bird, has preserved its colours wonderfully. In the Bosporan kingdom, the population of which lived by agriculture and vine-growing, the cult of the goddess of fertility, Demeter, was particularly widespread. The Bolshaya Bliznitsa burial mound on the Taman peninsula, where in stone vaults decorated with murals were buried priestesses of Demeter, became famous due to the truly incredible riches found there; one of the priestesses' dresses alone was embellished with more than two thousand

The Venus of Tauris.
1st – 2nd century Roman copy of a Greek original (300 – 200 B.C.)

The Phanagorian Sphinx.
500 — 400 B.C.

gold plaques. The gold crowns, earrings, bracelets and other exquisitely made decorative objects are kept in the **Gold Room** of the Hermitage, the remainder in **room 116**, case 30. From the ancient Bosporan graves were extracted silver and bronze utensils and excellent examples of Attic vases **(rooms 116** and **117)**. A well preserved antique sarcophagus of cypress and boxwood, with carved designs and traces of blue and red paint, was found in one of the stone vaults of the Yuz-Oba mound near Kerch **(room 117)**. Also of interest is a group of objects from a late royal tomb dating from the third century A.D. **(room 116**, case 32 and the **Gold Room)**, in which of particular note are a gold mask, apparently representing the Bosporan ruler Rhescuporis, and a large silver dish, a gift to a Bosporan king from the Roman emperor Caracalla. At the end of the third and beginning of the fourth centuries, the Bosporan kingdom was destroyed by the Goths.

Room 120. Nymphaeum, 600 B.C.—3rd century A.D. The small Bosporan town of Nymphaeum, which traded with Athens in corn, was founded by inhabitants of the island of Samos in the sixth century B.C. on the site of a Scythian settlement. Excavations carried out by a Hermitage scientific expedition discovered dug-outs dating back to Scythian times with fragments of earthenware and the remains of grains of wheat and barley. Of great interest and importance was the discovery of a Greek shrine dedicated to the goddess Demeter. Many terracotta statuettes were found here, as well as goblets, rhytons, jugs of local and Attic origin brought by the natives of Nymphaeum as a gift to the gods, and some finely made terracotta acroteria and parts of a cornice. At the entrance to the shrine was a stone bearing the Greek inscription: "Do not befoul the shrine".

Room 100 contains relics from Olbia (600 B.C.—3rd century A.D.) and from Chersonesus (500 B.C.—4th century A.D.). Olbia, one of the colonies belonging to Miletus founded in the sixth century B.C. on the banks of the Bug estuary, was an important trading town which supplied Greece with corn.

Excavations led to the discovery of a fortress wall, the ruins of houses and temples, artisan quarters, potteries, wineries and bakeries. In Olbia there have been found relics of Greek writing (funeral and dedicative texts), works of art, Olbian bronze coins and various other articles.

The Tauric Chersonesus, three kilometres west of Sevastopol, was founded by Greeks in the fifth century B.C., and excavations have been carried out on the site of the ancient town from 1888 up to the present day. Displayed in the exhibition are ceramics, architectural details, coins, relics of writing and sculptures.

The Art and Culture of Ancient Italy and Rome: 700 B.C.—4th century A.D.
Ground floor, rooms 102, 106, 107, 127—131

Rooms 130 and 131. Italian culture, 700—100 B.C., was the basis upon which grew up the antique culture of the slave-owning society of Rome. The exhibition in **room 130** (the Hall of Twenty Columns) opens with a section devoted to the art of Etruria, the most important region of ancient Italy, which reached its apogee in the seventh and sixth centuries B.C. The majority of the items in the Hermitage come from Etruscan tombs. Here note especially the distinctly original pieces of Etruscan ceramics—pitchers, amphoras, some fancy-shaped vessels, and enormous pots for wine on tall stands. The smooth, clean form and brilliant surface give these *buccheri* (articles made of smoked clay) the appearance of being made of metal (table 1, cabinets 4 and 33). The Etruscans excelled in the technique of processing metal, for example bronze, and this is seen from two superb specimens, the head of a lion made in the sixth century B.C. and a fifth century figure of a youth. The latter is a cinerary urn, representing a reclining figure, in the conventional pose of a person taking food at table. The muscles of the body are emphasized, and the classically proportioned face wears an expression of calm. The head of the lion is a fragment of one of those statues that were placed at the entrance to the burial vaults of the nobility in order to drive away evil spirits. The display also includes some bronzeware of the sixth and fifth centuries B.C., notably statuettes, bronze mirrors, a bowl with a handle in the form of a Triton, and a tripodal censer with an open-work frieze. Etruscan terracotta is represented by some third and second century cinerary urns in the form of small boxes, with a relief on the outer wall and the reclining figure of the deceased on the lid. The exhibition also possesses copious examples of the ceramics produced in the Greek towns situated in Campagna, Lucania, Apulia and Calabria. Of wide renown is the black-lacquered hydria adorned with a relief that has kept its gilt and traces of colour. Found in the nineteenth century in the town of Cumae, it has been called the Regina Vasorum on account of its beauty of form and richness of decoration.

Towards the end of the third century B.C., one by one all the provinces of Italy were brought under the subjection of Rome.

Room 127. Ancient Rome, 1000 B.C.—early 1st century A.D. The distinctive feature of Roman art was the sculptural portrait. Roman sculptors, whose names are unknown to us, portrayed in marble with great realism their contemporaries: statesmen, philosophers, emperors, military leaders, and distinguished Roman men and women. Assembled in the Hermitage are around one hundred and twenty portraits **(rooms 106, 107, 127, 128)**. This superb collection makes it possible to trace the development of Roman portraiture over a period of almost four hundred years. Belonging to the late period of the republic (second and first

Bronze cinerary urn. Etruria, 500 – 400 B.C.

centuries B.C.), when portraiture became an independent genre, is the
bronze bust of a Roman (No. 229), two male marble portraits (Nos. 181,
183a), and the portrait of a woman (No. 138a). Each of them has a characteristic simplicity and is a faithful and accurate reproduction of the appearance of the model; in the past marble portraits were tinted, which gave
them even greater expressiveness. The statue of the emperor Octavian
Augustus seated on a throne (first century A.D.) is a typical example of
an official portrait from the time of the Empire. Found in Cumae, the
statue was made during the last years of Augustus' life; he is portrayed,
however, as a young man of athletic build (at the very time when the
Roman historian Suetonius was writing about the frailty of his body).
The individual features of the face are smoothed over, and the hair is
conveyed with great accuracy in the way that Roman sculptors loved.
The emperor is portrayed half-naked; in one hand he is holding a sceptre
and in the other the figure of the winged goddess Victory. It was in this

7*

manner that the ancient Greeks depicted Zeus, and the Romans Jupiter, their chief deity. Such deific portrayals of the emperor stood in Roman temples, public buildings and on city squares.

At the time of the Empire relief sculpture occupied a prominent place in the decoration of palaces, triumphal arches and columns. Displayed here is a marble slab with a relief design composed of laurel garlands and bucrania. The slab is a fragment of either an altar or a temple wall. In the horizontal cases are some Roman intaglios and cameos of the first three centuries A.D. with representations of the emperor and members of his family, and also of mythological scenes.

Room 129. Roman craft work and decorative art. By the window is displayed a large third century mosaic made of smalt and coloured stone, which in the past paved the floor of the *thermae* containing public baths and all kinds of rooms used for the recreation of the body and the mind. It illustrates the Greek myth of the youth Hylas, a companion of Jason, who, while the *Argo* was at anchor, went to a spring for water and was carried to the bottom by nymphs. Upon wall-brackets are fragments of mosaics which also decorated floors of Roman buildings.

Representing the work of the Roman crafts are articles made of glass, bronzes and ceramics, displayed in cabinets. In the first century B.C. Roman craftsmen mastered the production of blown glass, and this became a regular feature of everyday life (see the vessels for wine, fragrant oil and rouge, and the cinerary urns). Coloured glass was particularly highly valued. Roman ceramic vessels were made in red lacquer technique, with a delicate relief design produced by means of stamping. The red-lacquer vessels are notable for their perfection of form, many of them made so as to resemble metal vessels—see the small jug with a vine pattern.

Room 128. Roman art and everyday life. Individual exhibits introduce to us the architectural decoration of Roman buildings, among them fragments of murals from Pompeii, the marble capitals of columns, and an ornamental relief. In the horizontal cases by the windows are household articles, working tools and relics of writing. In the centre of the room is the Kolyvan vase (see the description on page 32).

Room 107. Roman sculpture, late 1st—early 4th centuries A.D. The enormous statue of Jupiter, 3.47 metres high (11 ft. 4.2 in.), is an

Statue of Octavian Augustus. 1st century A.D.

Portrait of Gaius Caesar.
Rome, 1st century A.D.

example of the monumental temple sculpture of the mid-first century:
it was found in the country villa of the emperor Domitian. The figure of
Jupiter is made of marble, and the clothing originally of gilded wood,
but during restoration work this was replaced by plaster. In the past,
gilt not only covered the surfaces of the raiments and other attributes
(the statuette of the goddess Victory and the staff), but also the locks
of hair and the beard.

Typical of Roman art is the portrayal of a Roman in a toga, the orator
with his arm outstretched addressing the people. One of the Hermitage
pieces (No. 173) is an example of this type of sculpture.

In Roman art the narrative relief was widespread, including the
depiction of military campaigns, battles, triumphal processions and
mythological tales. Of this type there are the reliefs on marble sarcophagi

Portrait of Emperor
Philip the Arabian. Rome,
3rd century A.D.

dating from the second and third centuries A.D. One of them is decorated with scenes from the Greek tragedy *Hippolytus*, another with stories of the Trojan war, and the relief on the third sarcophagus reproduces the ritual of a Roman wedding.

An important place in the exhibition is occupied by Roman portraiture, the apogee of which came in the second and third centuries A.D. Among the masterpieces of the Hermitage collection we should first of all mention the portrait of an unknown Roman (No. 187), the portrait of a youth (No. 213), the head of a Syrian woman (No. 205), the portraits of the emperors Lucius Verus, Philip the Arabian, Balbinus and the empress Salonina, and the portrait of a Roman woman (No. 223). The Roman sculptors of the second and third centuries, not confining themselves to a realistic representation of man's external appearance, strove to reveal his inner world. They were in fact the originators of the psychological portrait.

In **room 106** are displayed some large heads, fragments of colossal statues, representing captive Dacians with their hands bound, which adorned the forum of Trajan in Rome. The Roman Empire waged a continuous war of conquest, and such triumphal monuments were supposed to confirm in the minds of the people the invincibility of Roman military strength.

THE DEPARTMENT
OF WESTERN EUROPEAN ART

The collections in the department of Western European art, the oldest in the Hermitage, are notable for their exceptional richness. They include paintings, sculptures, drawings and engravings, various items of applied art, coins and medals from different countries.

At the present time the following exhibitions are open to view:

Western European Applied Art: 11th-15th centuries.
Italian Art: 13th-18th centuries.
Spanish Art: 16th-17th centuries.
Art of the Netherlands: 15th-16th centuries.
Flemish Art: 17th century.
Dutch Art: 17th century.
German Art: 15th-18th centuries.
French Art: 15th-20th centuries.
English Art: 17th-19th centuries.
Art of European Countries and of the United States of America: 19th-20th centuries.
Western European Arms and Armour: 15th-17th centuries.
Western European Tapestries: 15th-18th centuries.
Western European Carved Stone: 12th-19th centuries.
Western European Porcelain: 18th-20th centuries.
Western European Jewellery: 16th-19th centuries (Gold Room).

Western European Applied Art: 11th—15th centuries
First floor, room 259

The exhibition presents relics of art dating back to feudal times from different Western European countries. In the Hermitage Museum there are some excellent, and in many cases unique examples of Romanesque and Gothic styles, made by craftsmen whose names are now unknown.

The ecclesiastic, religious character of the culture of medieval society is reflected in both the style and the function of the items displayed in the exhibition.

The coins (case 1) help us to re-create the motley political map of feudal Europe. The most interesting are the coins of the barbaric kingdoms which arose on the ruins of the Roman Empire, the denarii from the times of Charlemagne, king of the Franks, and his successors the Carlovingians, coins of the French duchies of Normandy, Aquitaine and Touraine, German bracteates bearing the images of feudal ecclesiastics, coins of the conquerors of Sicily—the Normans, and the currency units of Western European possessions in the East—the principality of Antioch, the province of Tripolitania and the kingdom of Jerusalem which were formed as a result of the holy crusades.

In a number of cabinets are displayed items of church-plate, the work of twelfth and thirteenth century goldsmiths and silversmiths. The reliquary in the form of the figure of a deacon is a unique work of Romanesque style, made in France in the twelfth century. This statuette, intended for preserving holy relics, was produced by beating thin, gilded silver plate on to a wooden core, and it is embellished with filigree and semiprecious stones. The fine workmanship of the facial features of the figure is particularly striking.

A typical example of French Gothic art is the large, thirteenth century processional cross bearing the figures of Christ, the Virgin Mary and the apostle John, and adorned with a delicately made design consisting of oak and vine leaves.

There are a great many examples in the exhibition of *champlevé* enamel on copper, for which the French city of Limoges was famous in the twelfth and thirteenth centuries. Most of these are reliquaries in the form of caskets with roof-shaped lids, or figures of the Madonna, decorative panels for facing altars, ornamental book mounts, basins for washing the hands, and candlesticks. Remarkable for the freshness of the colours and the virtuosity of its workmanship is the twelfth century casket with the representation of scenes from the life of Sainte Valérie, the patroness of the city of Limoges (case 6).

In the Middle Ages the art of ivory carving came to be widely practised. The twelfth century walrus ivory chessmen (case 3) are among the

Reliquary in the form of the figure
of a deacon. France, 12th century

few extant articles pertaining to secular life. Among the fourteenth century household objects there are some jewellery caskets, knives with ivory handles, and shallow boxes for keeping mirrors (cabinet 16, cases 2 and 9). In the small French sculptures (cabinet 16), the majority of which depict the Virgin whose cult was widespread in the Middle Ages, it is possible to trace the transition from the Romanesque style to the Gothic. In the thirteenth century figure of the seated Virgin there are still many features of Romanesque style: it is heavy, stiff and somewhat primitively executed. Next to it the fourteenth century Gothic statuette appears light and full of life; the Virgin is standing, her torso leaning back slightly, and a conventional smile animates her face. At one time the sculpture was brightly painted and gilded in parts. Two cabinets contain an interesting collection of grotesquely shaped bronze water ewers, so-called aquamaniles, that came into use in the twelfth century for the ritual washing of the priest's hands during Mass (see the figure of a horseman, a knight fighting a dragon, and others).

Medieval ceramics are represented by some Hispano-Moresque lustre ware from Málaga and Valencia. Outstanding among these examples is the famous "Fortuny Vase", named after the Spanish painter Fortuny who found it in 1871 in the village of Salar near Granada. This fourteenth century vase, made for the palace of Alhambra in the potteries of Málaga, is the earliest of the decorative objects from Alhambra that have been preserved. The fine artistic quality and the exceptionally good state of preservation ensure a special place for the "Fortuny Vase" among the ceramics in the museum.

On display in the exhibition are also some medieval fabrics, embroideries, weapons, furniture and stained glass.

Western European Arms and Armour: 15th—17th centuries
First floor, room 243

The fine collection of fifteenth to seventeenth century Western European weapons in the Hermitage comprises several thousand items. The exhibition is divided into two sections: along the wall opposite the windows and in the centre of the room are different pieces of arms which illustrate the evolution of weaponry; beside the windows on display boards and in horizontal cases are concentrated the examples of weaponry, made in France, Italy, Spain and Germany, most perfect from the point of view of artistic decoration.

At the beginning of the first section is diplayed a stand of arms of a knight—a sword, spear, dagger, chain-mail, and the plate-armour which replaced it in the early fifteenth century. Fifteenth century Gothic armour, with pointed contours, consisted of separate metal plates fastened together by straps. Such a suit of armour would number up to one hundred and sixty plates, and its weight ranged between sixteen and twenty kilograms (35 to 44 lbs.). Sixteenth century armour, the appearance of which is associated with the name of the German emperor

SIMONE MARTINI.
Madonna. 1339—42

Maximilian, was lighter than the Gothic, more comfortable and affording greater freedom of movement, and the corrugated surface, by causing the opponent's sword to glide off, softened the blow.

In the middle of the room are mounted suits of war harness for man and horse dating back to the sixteenth century. This cavalcada re-creates the appearance of a company of knights ready for battle or for a tournament.

The invention of firearms brought about the attempt, by making it thicker, to create armour of reinforced strength, the weight of which now came to forty kilograms. Such armour was delivered to the customer by the gunsmith after a trial shooting with a musket at a distance of one hundred paces (see the breastplate with the bullet mark, the sign that it has been tested). However, troops of knights could not withstand the guns of the townspeople, and together with feudal knighthood their armour too disappeared from the historical scene. The forerunner of the musket was the arbalest, a variety of cross-bow, the string of which was pulled by means of a special mechanism (cabinet 17). The bolt, a short, heavy arrow, when shot from the arbalest would pierce a knight's armour at a distance of seventy-five paces.

Very interesting are the peasant weapons, the shape of which goes back to the simplest working tools. These include the fighting scythe, whip and flail known as the Morgenstern. The name of this weapon — "morning star" — probably stems from the fact that its spikes resemble the points of a star. Another possible explanation may be that the insurgent peasants whose main weapon it was usually attacked the enemy suddenly, by the early light of dawn.

Italian Art: 13th—18th centuries
First floor,
rooms 207—222, 226—238 and 241

The exhibition of thirteenth to eighteenth century Italian art occupies over thirty rooms. All the important Italian schools of art are represented by works of the most eminent exponents of painting and sculpture, and also by items of applied art.

Italy was the first European country to set foot upon the path of progressive social and cultural achievement. In Italian cities, amid the fierce struggle against the medieval, feudal way of life, a new bourgeois culture developed. It was distinguished by its secular, optimistic character and was imbued with a belief in the reason and potentiality of man. Both literature and art reached a high peak. This new stage in the development of Western European culture became known as the age of the Renaissance.

Room 207. The art of the 13th—14th centuries. The first room in the exhibition contains works of art created in different Italian towns. The earliest of these is the *Crucifixion* by the Pisan artist Ugolino da Tedici, a very rare example of the painting of the second half of the thirteenth century.

The finest item in the room is the work of one of the foremost Italian artists of the fourteenth century, Simone Martini (1283—1344), who

LEONARDO DA VINCI. The Benois Madonna. 1478

LEONARDO DA VINCI. The Litta Madonna. *C.* 1490

hailed from Siena. He depicts the Madonna in a scene from the Annunciation,* when she humbly listens to the word of the angel. The lithe, elongated figure of the Madonna, smoothly wrapped in a blue cloak reaching down to the ground, stands out sharply against a gold background. Finely executed and beautiful in its colours, the painting has an unusual poetic quality.

The exhibition includes a number of works by the Florentine artists Spinello Aretino, Lorenzo da Niccolo Gerini and Antonio Firenze. In **rooms 208—216** is represented chiefly the Florentine school of painting, which in the fifteenth century assumed the leading role among the Italian schools of art. In rooms situated parallel to these **(217—222)** are examples of the art of another important school, the Venetian.

Rooms 208—213. The fifteenth century, the so-called Early Renaissance, was marked by persistent quests and important discoveries in several different spheres. Artists worked out the laws of perspective, developed the theory of the proportions of the human body, acquired new methods of composition and studied the legacy of antiquity. In their works they strove to convey the richness of the world around them, making man the focal point of interest.

Room 209. The fresco entitled *Madonna and Child with St Dominic and St Thomas Aquinas* was painted at the beginning of the 1440s on the refectory wall in the monastery of San Domenico in the township of Fiesole, near Florence, by the artist and monk Fra Beato Angelico da Fiesole (1387—1455), and is a good example of how in art the old is replaced by the new. The figures have acquired a three-dimensional quality, the faces have an individuality of their own, and the gold background has been replaced by a blue sky. Skilfully represented is the gossamery fabric of the cloak falling from the shoulder of the Madonna, whose whole appearance is filled with tranquillity, contemplation and a gentle beauty.

The Vision of St Augustine acquaints us with the work of the famous fifteenth century Florentine painter, Filippo Lippi (1406—1469). Taking a religious theme, the artist depicted his figures against a landscape back-

---

* The Hermitage painting is a panel from the diptych. Its other panel depicting Archangel Gabriel is housed in the National Gallery, Washington.

ground, using methods of linear perspective. The new view of man in the age of the Renaissance brought about the appearance of the realistic portrait. Interesting in this respect is the bronze bust of an unknown man by Sperandio Savelli (1425—1495), and similarly the terracotta *Portrait of a Florentine Man* by Benedetto da Maiano (1442—1497), exhibited in **room 210** where fifteenth century Florentine sculpture is displayed. Among these items is the *Nativity* (majolica) by Giovanni Della Robbia (1469—1529). This is notable for the narrative character typical of the Early Renaissance, and resembles an everyday scene portrayed with a lively spontaneity. The development of the use of majolica is connected with the studio of the famous Florentine sculptor, Luca Della Robbia (1400—1481), who was ranked by contemporaries as one of the great innovators. This same room contains a terracotta bust of his entitled the *Infant John the Baptist* and the wall medallions bearing figures in relief. The work of two of the leading sculptors of the Florentine Renaissance, Antonio Rossellino and Mino da Fiesole, is represented by marble reliefs depicting the Madonna and Child (**rooms 211 and 212**).

Room 212. The *Annunciation* by the Venetian Cima da Conegliano (1459—1517) is a typical painting of the Early Renaissance. The artist fixes the attention of the observer not only upon the figures of the Madonna and the angel, but also upon individual details, for example a fly crawling across the paper. The *Portrait of a Woman* by the Ferrarese painter Lozenzo Costa (1460—1535) is a beautiful example of the half-length portrait, which was widespread in the fifteenth century. Among several works by the Bolognese artist Francesco Francia (1450—1517/18) the richly coloured *Madonna and Child with St Lawrence, St Jerome and Two Angels* is worthy of special note. The traditional solemnity is combined in this altar-painting with a convincing characterization of the figures.

In **room 213** we should single out two late canvases, *St Dominic* and *St Jerome*, by Sandro Botticelli (1444/45—1510). Among the works displayed here there is also one of the finest paintings in the Hermitage collection, the *Adoration of the Child* by Filippino Lippi (1457?—1504). Also here are *St Sebastian* and *Portrait of a Young Man* by the Umbrian Pietro Perugino. The Florentine sculptor Desiderio da Settignano (1428—1464) is represented by two marble heads of the infant Christ.

RAPHAEL. The Conestabile Madonna. 1500

Room 214. The achievements of the fifteenth century are summed up in the work of Leonardo da Vinci (1452—1519), which opened up a new era in the development of Italian art—the High Renaissance. Little over ten of the great master's paintings have survived and these are dispersed among museums of different countries. There are two Leonardos in the Soviet Union, both housed in the Hermitage.

The *Benois Madonna*, sometimes called the *Madonna with a Flower*, was painted about 1478. Rejecting the traditional representation of the Madonna, Leonardo created an exalted female figure full of terrestrial charm. The smiling, youthful Madonna, in the smart dress of a Florentine townswoman, is holding a flower in front of the child, watching the still uncertain movements of the boy who is reaching out for the petals. The mist (*sfumato*), typical of Leonardo's work, lends the faces an unusual expressiveness. The sturdy, plump body of the boy, modelled in chiaroscuro, is evidence of the fact that the discoveries of Leonardo the scientist aided Leonardo the artist; it was not without cause that he called painting a science, "the legitimate child of nature". The theme of the glorification of man, of great emotions, is felt even more strongly in the *Litta Madonna*, which was painted around 1490. The sublime and poetic image combining physical and spiritual beauty embodies the Renaissance ideal. Leonardo portrayed with wonderful skill the delicate body of the child, the golden ringlets of his hair and the intent gaze turned towards the spectator. The serene silhouette of the Madonna stands out boldly against the dark background of the wall; the bright openings of the windows, beyond which stretches a mountain landscape shrouded in a bluish haze, are placed symmetrically at each side and, balancing the composition, create an illusion of space. Because of the perfection of formal arrangement characteristic of the High Renaissance, this work of Leonardo evokes a feeling of tranquillity, calm and harmony.

Among the works exhibited in **room 215** of pupils and disciples of Leonardo—Andrea del Sarto, Cesare da Sesto, Bernardino Luini and Salaino—there is one painting which stands out in particular for its great artistic quality. This is the *Portrait of a Woman*, also known as *Columbine* or *Flora*, painted by Francesco Melzi, a young friend of Leonardo. To a certain extent the head of the Parmesan school, Antonio Correggio (1494—1534), was also influenced by Leonardo; the *Portrait of a Woman*

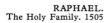

RAPHAEL.
The Holy Family. 1505

gives us some idea of his work. What takes the eye in **room 216** is the profoundly dramatic *Lamentation* signed by Sebastiano del Piombo (1485—1547), a well-known artist who worked in Venice and Rome. Extremely typical of the art of the Renaissance is the *Portrait of a Man* by a Venetian artist of the first half of the sixteenth century, Domenico Mancini, who created the ideal image of the man of his epoch, — outwardly perfect, spiritually rich, and self-confident.

Already in the 1530s there sprang up in Florence, and then became widespread in other Italian cities and abroad, a movement known as Mannerism, which marked a departure from the humanistic traditions of Renaissance art. Among the leading representatives of this trend are, in painting, the Florentine artists Jacopo Pontormo (1494—1557) and Giovanni Battista Rosso (1494—1540); and in sculpture, Giovanni da

MICHELANGELO.
Crouching Boy. Early 1530s

Bologna (1529—1608). Displayed in **room 216** are a fountain sculpture and some small bronzes of his.

Room 229. Raphael Santi (1483—1520), in whose works the ideals of the High Renaissance received their most lucid expression, is represented in the Hermitage by two early works. The *Conestabile Madonna* was painted by Raphael between 1500 and 1502. The young mother is pensively looking at a book, to which the child is reaching out; the Madonna's pure, lyrical appearance is echoed by a gentle spring landscape. In the *Holy Family* (1505) Raphael attained the majestic simplicity, clarity and harmony characteristic of the High Renaissance.

In the centre of the room is the fountain sculpture entitled *Dead Boy on a Dolphin* created by Lorenzo Lorenzetto after a drawing of Raphael. The theme of the sculpture, borrowed from a classical legend, describes how a dolphin bore his dead young friend ashore.

Another pupil of Raphael, the famous artist and architect Giulio Romano, produced an enormous cartoon *Procession with Elephants*, which appeared as part of a series of twenty-two representing the feats of the ancient Roman military leader Scipio Africanus and his triumphal procession after his victory in the Second Punic War.

The Hermitage possesses a rare collection of sixteenth century Italian majolica from various centres—Faenza, Siena, Castel-Durante, Deruta, Gubbio and Urbino. The majority of these items are decorative vessels —vases, bowls, dishes—with brightly coloured painted designs based upon motifs from classical and biblical legends. Particular mention should be made of a collection of fifteenth and sixteenth century Italian furniture which was made chiefly from walnut, decorated with carving and in many cases painted and gilded. A typical item of furniture was the *cassone*, a coffer used for keeping part of a bride's outfit. In their shape these coffers remind us of the sarcophagi of antiquity.

Room 227. Raphael's loggias. The museum contains the reproduction in the original size of Raphael's celebrated loggias, erected in the Vatican Palace by the architect Donato Bramante (1444—1514) and painted between 1516 and 1518 by pupils of Raphael after his sketches and under his supervision. The Hermitage copy was made at the end of the eighteenth century by a group of artists under Christopher Unterberger. The work of copying was carried out in the Vatican. Painted canvases were brought to St Petersburg, stretched out on frames and inserted into the walls of the Hermitage loggias specially built for this purpose by Giacomo Quarenghi.

Room 230. The work of the great sculptor, painter and architect Michelangelo (1475—1564) is represented in the Soviet Union by one sculpture, the *Crouching Boy*, created in the early 1530s and belonging apparently to the sculptures which were intended to adorn the tomb of a Medici in Florence. The statue remained unfinished; though we feel in it great inner strength, —a feature characteristic of the work of Michelangelo, —it cannot give one a comprehensive idea of the great master's art. Into the walls of the room have been fitted some frescoes by artists of the Raphaelite school.

Displayed in **room 217** is one of the great treasures of the Hermitage collection of Venetian painting, — *Judith* by Giorgione (1478?—1510), with whose work began the period of the High Renaissance in Venice. In his representation of the biblical heroine Judith, who slayed the enemy leader Holofernes, Giorgione created a noble, somewhat enigmatic in its restraint, but highly emotional and charming image of a young woman. Judith stands in a majestic pose, her sword lowered, her foot resting upon the severed head of her enemy. In 1968 the painting was restored; after the removal of the dirt and the varnish which had decomposed with age, Giorgione's colours sparkled like gems.

Room 219—221. Titian (1485/90—1576), the head of the Venetian school, began his creative work at the same time as Giorgione. With the exception of the *Flight into Egypt* (early 1500s), one of his early paintings, Titian is represented in the Hermitage by works from his mature period (*Portrait of a Young Woman, c.* 1530s; *Danaë*, painted in the 1550s; *Madonna and Child with Mary Magdalene, c.* 1560; *The Penitent Magdalene*, 1560s; *Christ Blessing*, 1560s; *Christ Carrying the Cross*, or *Christ and Simon of Cyrene*, 1560; and *St Sebastian, c.* 1570). *Danaë* was painted

LORENZO LORENZETTI. Dead Boy on a Dolphin

GIORGIONE. Judith. *C.* 1504

on the theme of the classical Greek myth in which Zeus, in the form of golden rain, visits his beloved, the princess Danaë, who is imprisoned in a tower. The painting is based upon the colour contrast of the nacre-pink body with the cold tone of the white sheet and the purple canopy of the bed. The perfect proportions of Danaë's naked body are evidence of Titian's adoption of the classical ideal of beauty.

In the *Penitent Magdalene* the artist focuses attention not on the ascetic idea of the Christian legend, but on the figure of the sensually beautiful young woman. The agitated state of Magdalene is echoed in the landscape, with the summer lightning aglow in the dark blue, thundery sky and the solitary tree bending against the gusts of wind. Toward the end of his life, in connection with the general crisis in Renaissance culture, some tragic notes are sounded in Titian's work. *St Sebastian*, painted by Titian at a very advanced age, strikes the viewer with the strength of its dramatic effect and the amazing artistic skill, evidence of the inexhaustible creative energy of this great Venetian painter.

Room 222. Acquainting us with the work of Paolo Veronese (1528—1588), one of the most eminent Venetian painters of the second half of the sixteenth century, is a group of excellent pictures: the vivid, jubilant *Adoration of the Magi*; the *Lamentation*, dramatic in spirit and expressive in colour; *Portrait of a Man*; and *Diana*, a small sketch made for the decorative paintings of the Villa Maser near Vicenza.

In two small rooms adjoining **room 222** there is a collection of Venetian glass and painted enamels on copper, Italian fabrics, and articles made of bronze and leather (fifteenth—seventeenth centuries).

Room 237. Side by side with Veronese's painting, *The Conversion of Saul*, dominated by a mood of perturbation and anxiety, in this room there is the only work of Jacopo Tintoretto (1518—1594) in the Hermitage collection, *The Birth of John the Baptist*. In this painting the genre subject appears as a distinct form, —women are fussing around the new-born child, and their dresses, the décor of the room, the cat creeping towards the hen, and the brazier on the floor, all take the spectator into the atmosphere of a sixteenth century Venetian house.

The Hermitage has a very large collection of paintings by artists of the Bologna Academy. Two canvases, *Holy Women at the Sepulchre* and *Lamentation over the Dead Christ*, introduce us to the work of the head of

TITIAN. Danaë. 1550s

the Bologna Academy, Annibale Carracci (1560—1609). The prominent representatives of the academic style were Guido Reni (*Girlhood of the Virgin* and *St Joseph Holding the Infant Christ*), Domenichino (*Mary Magdalene's Ascension into Heaven*) and Guercino (*The Martyrdom of St Catherine* and *The Assumption*). A number of paintings by the artists mentioned here are to be found in **room 231**.

Lionello Spada (1576—1622), having studied at first under Annibale Carracci, later became a disciple of Caravaggio. The fierce dramatic effect of his *Crucifixion of St Peter* derives not so much from the subject itself, as from his interpretation of it and from the use of sharp light and shade contrasts which he learned from Caravaggio.

Room 232. *The Lute Player*, the only painting in the Soviet Union by Michelangelo Merisi da Caravaggio (1573—1610), belongs to the early period of the artist's work. A young Italian, with a simple but expressive face, is pensively running his fingers over the strings of a lute. The brightly lit figure of the boy and the small accessories of still life

TITIAN.
The Penitent Magdalene.
Between 1566 and 1570

—a vase filled with flowers, fruit, a violin and music—stand out against a dark background. Caravaggio's work exercised great influence upon the development of realism, not only in Italian art but also abroad. It expressed the progressive tendencies in Italian art during the Baroque era (late sixteenth century to mid-eighteenth), which witnessed very diverse and contradictory artistic phenomena. The foremost artist of the Roman Baroque, the sculptor and architect Gianlorenzo Bernini (1598—1680), is represented by a *Self-portrait* in terracotta and by a splendid collection of terracotta *bozzetti*—small models for his monumental works.

Rooms 233—235 contain an exhibition of seventeenth and eighteenth century Italian art. In **room 233** there are works by representatives of the Genoese school of Baroque painting—Strozzi, Magnasco, Castiglione and others; in **room 234** there are paintings of the Neapolitan school,

VERONESE.
The Adoration of the Magi.
Early 1570s

while **room 235** contains works by artists of different schools—Crespi, Panini, Rotari, Torelli, etc. Eighteenth century Venetian painting is presented in rooms **236** and **238**. Three paintings—*Landscape, Town Scene,* and *View of a Square with a Palace*—are excellent examples of the work of Francesco Guardi (1712—1793), the celebrated creator of Venetian townscapes, full of light and air. A prominent place among the Venetian artists belongs to the brilliant pastellist Rosalba Carriera (1675—1757), whose work is displayed in **room 236**.

Exhibited in **room 238**, the so-called "Top-lighted Hall", are some large seventeenth and eighteenth century decorative paintings which once adorned palaces and churches. One of the leading artists of Italian Baroque was the Neapolitan Salvator Rosa (1615—1673), painter and etcher, the author of several paintings diverse in theme, imbued with

CARAVAGGIO. The Lute Player. 1595

great feeling, and pervaded with a romanticism of their own (*The Prodigal*, *Democritus and Prothagoras* and *Odysseus and Nausicaa*; in **room 234** is his *Portrait of a Man*). Another Neapolitan painter, Luca Giordano (1632—1705), nicknamed **Luca Fa Presto** ("Paint quickly", from the alleged habit of his father in urging ever greater speed), enjoyed great popularity both in Italy and abroad. His work is represented in the exhibition by some excellent canvases: *The Forge of Vulcan*, *The Centaurs' Fight with the Lapithae* and *The Dream of Bacchus*. The Bolognese painter Giuseppe Maria Crespi (1664—1747) achieved great expressiveness in his paintings by a skilful use of light and shade contrasts (see in **room 235** his *In the Cellar*, *Washerwoman*, *Woman Looking for Fleas* and *Self-portrait*, one of his best works). Also characteristic of Crespi's painting is the dramatic *Death of Joseph*, in which a realistic interpretation of the event is combined with a certain tinge of mysticism **(room 238)**. The full bloom of Venetian decorative painting in the eighteenth century is associated with the name of Giovanni Battista Tiepolo (1696—1770). Of the six large-scale canvases in the Hermitage collection five were painted by the artist for the Dolphino Palace in Venice, on themes from ancient Roman history—*Fabius Maximus Quintus in the Senate at Carthage*, *Coriolanus at the Walls of Rome*, *Mucius Scaevola before Porsenna*, *Cincinnatus Is Invited to Become Dictator* and *The Triumph of the Emperor*. These works display the special features of Tiepolo's painting, —his inexhaustible imagination, brilliant mastery of composition, and bold decorative sweep. In eighteenth century Venetian art there developed the genre of the *veduta* or townscape, the leading exponents of which were Antonio Canale (1697—1768), known as Canaletto, the author of the *Reception of the French Ambassador in Venice*, and Michele Marieschi (1710—1743). The views by these artists, animated by the figures of people, reproduce the architectural beauty of the "pearl of the Adriatic".

In the centre of the room stands the decorative sculpture entitled *The Death of Adonis* by Giuseppe Mazzuola (1644—1725). According to the myth, Adonis, the beloved of Venus, was torn to pieces by a wild boar while on a hunt. Here the sculptor skilfully conveys the turbulent movement, representing the moment when the frenzied beast attacks the youth. The sensation of vigour and energy is intensified by the brilliant working of the marble, calculated to reveal the play of light and shade.

In the second half of the eighteenth century Baroque was succeeded by Neoclassicism, which proclaimed the doctrine of unqualified adherence to antique exemplars. The main representative of Neoclassicism in Rome was Pompeo Batoni (1708—1787); his *Hercules between Love and Wisdom* is remarkable for the freshness of the colours and the calm grace of movement.

The Top-lighted Hall and the adjoining rooms are decorated with vases, candelabra and table-tops made by Russian craftsmen.

CANOVA. Hebe. 1801

Room 241 is devoted to the history of ancient painting. Its walls are adorned with large decorative panels which reproduce the development of ancient Greek painting as it suggested itself to the imagination of the nineteenth century artist on the basis of descriptions by the writers of antiquity. The panels were painted in encaustic on copper plates by the German artist Hiltensperger (1806—1890). The room contains a large collection of works by the leading figure in Italian classical sculpture, Antonio Canova (1757—1822)—*Orpheus, Cupid, Cupid's Kiss, Hebe*, and *Paris*. Also here is the work of another well-known sculptor of the Neoclassical school,—the Dane Bertel Thorwaldsen (1770—1844), including *Shepherd, Cupid with a Lyre* and *Portrait of the Countess Osterman-Tolstaya*.

Spanish Art: 16th—17th centuries
First floor, rooms 239 and 240

Room 240. The Hermitage collection of Spanish painting is one of the richest and most significant in the world. Among the sixteenth century paintings two works by Luis de Morales (1509?—1586), *Mater Dolorosa* and *Madonna and Child*, attract considerable attention. There is grimness and tragedy in the mournful, deliberately elongated faces of the Madonnas, while, as regards the colours, black-green and cold pink tones are predominant. To some extent the work of Morales reflected the religious, mystical mood of Spanish society created by the Catholic church, in those times extremely powerful in Spain. This fact was responsible for the continued prevalence of religious subjects in Spanish art.

One of the gems of the Hermitage picture gallery is *The Apostles Peter and Paul*, painted in 1614 by Domenikos Theotokopoulos (1541—1614), called El Greco on account of his Greek origin. In this work the artist portrays two complex characters, two conflicting natures. The expression on the face of Peter, the meek look in his dark, lustreless eyes, the slightly bowed figure, and the hand sagging beneath the weight of the key all reveal a contemplative, passive nature inclined to meditation and doubt. Paul is represented as a powerful, resolute personage; he has the high brow of a thinker, the feverishly fiery eyes of a fanatic, and his hand is resting authoritatively on the book. The inner tension of the figures, the disturbed folds of their robes, and the rich, glowing colours create an atmosphere of anxiety and spiritual exultation so characteristic of El Greco.

One of the leading Spanish artists of the late sixteenth and early seventeenth centuries was Francisco Ribalta (1551/58—1628), whose work is represented by the earliest of his dated paintings, *Raising of the Cross*, and a portrait of the great Spanish dramatist Lope de Vega. Portrait painting, for a long time the only form of the secular genre in Spain, is also represented by two canvases by Juan Pantoja de la Cruz (1551—1609).

Room 239. The seventeenth century, the "golden age" of Spanish national culture, produced a great galaxy of names: Cervantes, Lope de

9

EL GRECO.
The Apostles Peter
and Paul. 1614

Vega, Calderón and Tirso de Molina in literature, and in painting Velázquez, Ribera, Zurbarán and Murillo.

There are two paintings in the Hermitage by Diego de Silva Velázquez (1599—1660), one of the great masters of the past. From his early
period there is *Luncheon* (*c.* 1617), which portrays an old man and two
youths talking cheerfully and sitting in natural, relaxed postures at a
scantily laid table. In the figures of these common people certain features
of the Spanish national character are subtly observed—gaiety and restraint, open generosity and a certain severity. The still life is wonderfully painted; it consists of a glass containing golden wine, a herring
in an earthenware dish, a pomegranate, a turnip and a knife. The objects
cast a slight shadow on the table, which is covered with a white cloth.

Much of Velázquez's work was devoted to portrait painting. The *Portrait of Count Olivares* (*c.* 1638) is from the outside laconic, but contains deep characterization. The plump, coarse face, the savage look in the dark eyes, and the sensual smile reveal some peculiarities of the imperious and powerful statesman, the confident and minister of Philip IV. Velázquez's genius as a painter is clearly seen in the bold contours of the face, in the subtle rendering of shades in the black velvet of the cloak, and in the silvery, transparent air and light. Also in this room are paintings by pupils of Velázquez—Juan Mazo's *Portrait of Philip IV* and Juan Pareja's *Portrait of the Commander of the Order of Santiago de Compostela* —and by followers of his, Antonio Puga (*The Grinder*) and Antonio Pereda (*Still Life*).

MURILLO. The Assumption of
the Madonna. Between 1670
and 1680

Note also the work of Velázquez elder contemporary José Ribera
(1591—1652). His paintings *St Jerome Listening to the Sound of the
Trumpet* and *St Sebastian and St Irene* are remarkable for the intense
emotional quality of the figures, the saturation of colour, and the unusual
use of light and shade. The monumental canvas by Francisco de Zurbarán
(*c.* 1598—1664) entitled *St Lawrence* portrays one of the first deacons of
the church, who suffered martyrdom by being broiled on a gridiron
which he is represented in art as holding in his hand. Thickset, and with
a simple but inspired face, St Lawrence calls to mind the heroes of
Spanish folk tales. The figure of the saint, in a heavy velvet vestment
embroidered with gold, appears especially expressive set against the
background of a serene landscape with a low horizon. The work of Murillo
(1618—1682), a younger contemporary of Velázquez and Zurbarán, is

GOYA. Portrait of Antonia Zárate

illustrated by twelve paintings. His canvases on religious subjects—*Isaac Blessing Jacob*, *Rest on the Flight into Egypt* and *The Assumption*—are notable for the freeness of composition, the attractive representation of the figures of women and children, and the beautiful range of colours. The *Boy with a Dog* is an example of genre painting, often practised by Murillo and in which his talent as a realist painter is clearly seen.

The early nineteenth century art in Spain is represented by the *Portrait of the Actress Antonia Zárate* by Francisco de Goya (1746—1828).

Art of the Netherlands: 15th—16th centuries
First floor,
rooms 248, 258, 260—262

In the fifteenth and sixteenth centuries the Netherlands experienced the Renaissance. The small collection in the Hermitage allows the viewer to trace in the work of its leading masters the special features of the art of this period.

Room 261. One of the marvels of the collection is the small painting of the *Virgin and Child* by Robert Campin (1378/9—1444), who worked in the town of Tournai. In books on the history of art he was conventionally referred to as the Master with the Mousetrap, then as the Master of Mérode, and finally as the Master of Flémalle. In this work is revealed a new attitude on the part of the artist towards the world, whose beauty he strives to put down on canvas. With great care and thoroughness he reproduces the furniture of a room, the texture of objects; he lovingly depicts the landscape discernible beyond the window and the soft light which fills the interior, and in so doing attains such artistic perfection that his creation is placed among the finest examples of Renaissance art. Rogier van der Weyden (1400—1464) was one of the leading masters of the Netherlandish art. In his *St Luke Drawing the Virgin* the figures are placed in the foreground in an open loggia, beyond which stretches a landscape painted in great detail and flooded with light. Hugo van der Goes (died 1482) was one of the foremost painters of the second half of the fifteenth century. In his *Lamentation over the Dead Christ* and the

ROBERT CAMPIN. The Virgin and Child. 1430s

monumental triptych entitled *The Adoration of the Magi* the artist presents a dramatic interpretation of the events and draws his characters with genuine realist strength.

Room 260 contains the large altar-piece by Jan Provost, *The Virgin in Majesty*, which is in keeping with the traditions of religious painting. Also displayed in this room is a stone portal with a wooden door (from Liège), a carved wooden altar from Antwerp dated around 1500, and on the walls two tapestries — *The Flood* and *Noah's Sacrifice* (Brussels, 16th century).

Rooms 262 and 258. At the beginning of the sixteenth century landscape painting and the representation of scenes from everyday life already stood out in Netherlandish art as independent genres. Portrait painting was also widespread. Genre painting is illustrated by the works of the Antwerp artists Marinus van Reymerswaele (*The Moneychangers*) and Joachim Beuckelaer (*Village Feast*) and by the Amsterdam painter Pieter Aertsen (*Healing of the Sick*). Sixteenth century Netherlandish landscape painting is represented by the works of Joachim Patinier, Herri met de Bles, Jan de Cock, Adriaen Isenbrandt and the unknown, late sixteenth century Netherlandish artist, traditionally called the Master of the Winter Landscapes.

At the beginning of the sixteenth century a number of artists in the Netherlands came under the influence of Italian art. This may be observed if we examine the work of Jan Gossaert, Barent van Orley, Frans Floris, Michel van Coxcie and Lambert Lombard. The distinguished painter and engraver Lucas van Leyden (1494—1533), while assimilating Italian influences, was able to preserve a distinctive originality. The triptych in the Hermitage entitled *The Healing of the Blind Man of Jericho* is among the most famous of his works. Introducing us to the work of the great artist Pieter Bruegel the Elder is the painting *The Fair* (a copy made by the artist's son, Pieter Bruegel the Younger). The collection of portraits includes the *Portrait of a Man with a Carnation* by an unknown sixteenth century artist, two companion knee-length portraits by Frans Pourbus and two group portraits by Dirck Jacobsz.

The Netherlandish art of the fifteenth and sixteenth centuries was the basis upon which developed, in the seventeenth, two important national schools of painting — the Flemish and the Dutch.

RUBENS. The Union of Earth and Water. Between 1612 and 1615

RUBENS. Perseus and Andromeda. 1620—21

Flemish Art: 17th century
First floor, rooms 245—247

Room 247. The most prominent figure in the Flemish art of the
seventeenth century was Peter Paul Rubens (1577—1640), a many-sided
artist of great talent, the creator of celebrated paintings, and the teacher of
the leading Flemish artists. The Hermitage collection comprises twenty-
two paintings and nineteen sketches of Rubens, and there are some
excellent drawings of his in the section devoted to this branch of art.

In the small picture *The Statue of Ceres*, painted between 1612 and
1616, Rubens re-created on canvas the antique sculpture of the goddess
of growing vegetation he had seen in Rome. Beside the rough surface
of the ancient marble of the statue the painter placed the plump bodies of

the bustling cupids, who are adorning with heavy garlands of ripe fruit the niche containing the image of the goddess. And in this contrast lies the very essence of Rubens's creative work, in which he combined an assimilation of antique exemplars with an optimistic and impassioned perception of life. *The Union of Earth and Water*, painted between 1612 and 1615, is one of the finest of the artist's early works, in the conception of which the symbolic union of the goddess of the earth, Cybele, and Neptune, god of the sea, personifies peace and the prosperity of the state. The beauty of the large naked bodies, the rich colours, and the joyful view of the world transform Rubens's work into a jubilant song in praise of life. The *Descent from the Cross* (1612—1615) is an altar-piece painted for the Capuchin monastery at Lierre, near Antwerp.

In Rubens's monumental canvas, *Feast at the House of Simon the Pharisee*, painted about 1618 with the assistance of his talented pupil Van Dyck, there appears a whole gallery of striking types and characters. The focusing of the centre of interest to the right where both the main figures, Christ and the sinner, are portrayed, and the contrasting colours heightened the dramatic intensity of the story. The very treatment of the figures and the introduction of a number of details from everyday life lend this altar-painting a completely secular character.

Between 1618 and 1620 Rubens was drawn to dramatic themes, which he turned into compositions full of movement and passion. Characteristic of these works is the magnificent sketch *Lion Hunt* (*c.* 1618) for the painting which is in the Pinakothek in Munich. From 1622 to 1625 Rubens, commissioned by the French queen Marie de' Medici, created a cycle of paintings entitled *The Life of Marie de' Medici* for the decoration of the Luxembourg Palace in Paris. They are now in the Louvre. In the Hermitage there are five sketches made by Rubens himself for the cycle. The best of these is the *Coronation of Marie de' Medici*.

Dating from the period of 1629 to 1634 are the Hermitage sketches of two parts of the huge ceiling in the Banqueting House in the royal palace of Whitehall in England.

Rubens's landscape painting is represented by two pictures—an early work, *The Carters* (*c.* 1620), and a late one, *Rainbow Landscape* (1630).

The Hermitage painting *Perseus and Andromeda*, dated 1620—21, is very well known. Perseus, the hero of the ancient myth, freed the princess

Andromeda by killing the sea-monster to which she had been brought as a sacrifice. The painting represents the moment when the winged goddess of Glory crowns Perseus with a laurel wreath; at the feet of the victor lies the dead body of the monster, and Andromeda stands, her eyes lowered, before her rescuer. The charm of her naked body lies not in its classical austerity but in the throbbing life, in the warmth, and full-blooded roundness of form.

One of the masterpieces of the Hermitage collection is the *Portrait of a Lady of the Chamber* (1625), an unpretentious but charming portrayal of a girl in the full bloom of youth. The liquid fluency of brushstroke in this picture is remarkable even for Rubens. The paint, with one shade passing almost imperceptibly into the next, is like enamel, delicate and limpid, as though lit from the inside.

In 1634, on the occasion of the traditional entry into Antwerp of the new Spanish ruler, Rubens led the work of decorating the town for the celebrations. His sketches have been preserved. In *Mercury Leaving the City of Antwerp*, using the language of allegory, the painter speaks of the need to end the war which was disastrous for Flanders; *The Temple of Janus* is also devoted to this theme.

In the last years of his life Rubens painted his famous *Bacchus* (*c.* 1640). Rejecting the tradition according to which Bacchus was portrayed as a beautiful youth, the god of wine and merriment was represented by the great master as hearty and boisterous, in keeping with Flemish folk spirit. A warm, golden light envelops the figures and the distant hills and broad plains which stretch behind them, and against the background of this majestic landscape, the scene of the bacchanalia appears as the embodiment of the "mighty" element of nature.

Room 246. First place among the painters of the Flemish school after Rubens belongs to Anthony van Dyck (1599—1641). In the Hermitage there are twenty-five paintings, mainly portraits, illustrating different periods in the artist's work.

Already in his early canvases (*Portrait of Balthasarina van Linick*, *A Family Group*), we can discern the young artist's desire to convey the psychological condition of the human being and to gain insight into his inner world. Certain changes in Rubens's mode of expression were linked with his stay in Italy: the simplicity of the early works was replaced by

VAN DYCK. Self-portrait.
   Late 1620s — early 1630s

a more striking representation of his subject, a more subtle manner, in both the methods of painting and the compositional arrangement. Dating from the 1620s are the *Portrait of the Banker Antoine Lumagne* and the *Portrait of a Man*, formerly thought to be the Antwerp physician Lazarus Maharkijzus. Van Dyck's life was an unbroken series of triumphs. In his *Self-portrait* he appears before the spectator as a minion of fortune—sophisticated, charming and casually elegant. Well illustrated in the Hermitage is the latter period of the artist's work. His years in England (1632—41) were very successful, with immense prestige at the court of Charles I. He created a whole gallery of magnificent formal portraits of the English aristocracy. These include portraits of Charles I, Queen Henrietta Maria, Henry Danvers the Earl of Danby, Thomas Wharton and others.

JORDAENS. The Bean King. *C.* 1638

The Virgin with Partridges (*c.* 1632) is a typical Van Dyck composition on a religious theme, treated in the manner of a secular scene, and with that refinement and elegance which are the distinctive features of his individuality as an artist.

Room 245. Jordaens, Snyders, Brouwer, Teniers. Jacob Jordaens (1593—1678), who became, after the death of Rubens, the leading figure in the Flemish school, worked in several different genres.

He loved to employ as a basis for his paintings subjects associated with national customs. An excellent example of this is *The Bean King* (*c.* 1638), which portrays the traditional revel on Christmas eve. In this painting the vivid brush of Jordaens caught the unrestrained, somewhat vulgar mirth of a Flemish burgher family.

It seems that all the riches of the earth and of the depths of the sea are found in the amazing wealth of the paintings from the *Shops* series

SNYDERS. Fruit in a Bowl

by Frans Snyders (1579—1657). The picturesque heaps of fruits, vegetables, game and fish, displayed in an unusual array, set each other off
to great effect.

The vigorously energetic paintings of Paul de Vos (c. 1596—1678)
—*The Leopard Hunt*, *The Bear Hunt*, and *The Deer Hunt*—are examples
of a type of painting which was particularly popular among the Flemish
nobility, who used such pictures to decorate their hunting lodges.

Adriaen Brouwer (1606—1638) was a leading exponent of genre painting, which in seventeenth century Flemish art played a rather modest
role. The heroes of Brouwer's works are the representatives of the lower
strata of urban society and sometimes peasants (*Scene in a Tavern*, *The
Flute Player*, *Peasants in a Tavern*).

David Teniers the Younger (1610—1690), a pupil of Brouwer and a
popular genre and landscape painter, is represented by more than thirty

VOS. The Bear Hunt

canvases. Teniers, who often portrayed peasant life, chose idyllic scenes out in the country, festivals and weddings, rather than the working, everyday life of the village. His paintings, consistent in their silvery tones, are notable for their great artistic mastery.

Dutch Art: 17th century
First floor, rooms 249—257

The Hermitage collection of seventeenth century Dutch painting is famous throughout the world; the main exhibition is in **room 249**—the Tent Hall—where paintings by the leading masters in the different genres are displayed.

Jan van Goyen (1596—1656) is one of the outstanding landscape painters of the first half of the seventeenth century. A list of titles—*The Coast at Scheweningen, The Maas near Dordrecht, Winter Landscape near the Hague*—is enough to show that Goyen was inspired by his native countryside. His paintings are usually much greater in width than height, the sky occupying two thirds of the canvas with the horizon set low in the picture. This manner produces an extraordinary sense of space, emphasizing at the same time the flatness of the Dutch landscape. There are no bright colours in his paintings: they are almost monochromes. The fine gradation of grey and subdued yellow tones conveys the feeling of air saturated with moisture, softening the contours, and the further away the objects are the more indistinct their outlines become. This method, known as aerial perspective, was one of the splendid achievements of the Dutch school of painting.

Goyen's contemporary, Salomon van Ruisdael (1600—1670), is represented by an excellent canvas entitled *The Ferry*. The Hermitage collection, through the example of the works of Aert van der Neer, Pieter Nolpe, Jan Porcellis, Abraham Willaerts, etc., enables us to trace the development of Dutch landscape painting. The most successful landscape painter in the second half of the seventeenth century was Jacob van Ruisdael (1628/29—1682); there are eleven paintings by him in the Hermitage. One of his most celebrated works is the *Marsh* based on a romantic conception of nature, mighty and eternally reborn. *Peasant Cottages in the Dunes*, *Waterfall in Norway* and *Mountain Landscape* mark Jacob van Ruisdael as an artist capable of reproducing all the diversities of nature, her ever-changing appearance, with such profundity and feeling as was unknown previously in Dutch art.

Portrait, like landscape painting, is represented by the works of artists of different generations. The early canvases of Mierevelt and Ravesteyn, for the most part half-length portraits, are distinguished by the painstaking rendering of face and costume. The next period is illustrated by the work of Thomas de Keyser (1596—1667), the best-known portrait painter of his day. In his knee-length *Portrait of a Man* de Keyser creates the type of a Dutch burgher, business-like, self-confident, and prosperous. Belonging to this same period, the apogee of Dutch realistic art, is the work of Frans Hals (1580—1666). The two pictures in the Hermitage, *Portrait of a Young Man with a Glove in His Hand* (c. 1650) and *Portrait of a Man* (before 1660), are painted in a vigorous, robust manner, and with that ability to capture in his paintings fleeting impressions that distinguishes the brilliant talent of Hals.

Exceptionally rich is the collection of genre painting. Examples of the genre painting of the 1620s and 1630s are presented in the works of Dirck Hals, Willem Duyster and Jacob Duck, who portrayed groups of people making merry, tavern carousals, family concerts, card games, and everyday scenes, mainly from the lives of prosperous burghers and soldiers. Adriaen van Ostade (1610—1685), who for the most part portrayed peasants, occupies a special place among the genre painters. He is represented in the exhibition by paintings which are typical of his work generally: *The Scuffle*, *The Village Musicians*, four pictures from *The Five Senses* series, and others. The distinctive feature of the work of Jan Steen (1626—1679), one of the foremost Dutch painters of everyday life, is his fascinating anecdotal approach. The nine paintings by him in the Hermitage reflect his wide range of interests, and his humour and keen powers of observation in depicting scenes from the daily lives of the different strata of Dutch society (*The Smoker*, *The Marriage Contract*, *Physician Visiting a Sick Girl*, *The Revellers*, etc.). The artistic achievements of the Dutch genre painters of the second half of the seventeenth century can be seen clearly in the work of Pieter de Hooch (*A Lady and Her Servant*), Pieter Jansens (*A Room in a Dutch House*), Gabriel Metsu (*Breakfast*, *Physician Visiting a Sick Girl*), Frans Mieris (*Young Lady in the Morning*, *Breakfast with Oysters*) and Gerard Terborch (*A Glass of Lemonade*, *Reading a Letter*, and *Portrait of a Woman*). These artists, extolling in their paintings the mode of life of the upper layers of Dutch society, did not consider the subjects themselves of much importance; these are often repetitive and serve merely as a pretext for magnificent reproductions of items of furniture, clothing, and airy, brightly lit interiors.

Still-life painting came to be very widely practised in Holland during the seventeenth century. The artists convincingly reproduced the beauty of objects which surround us in our daily lives. Examples include the *Breakfast* paintings of Willem Claesz Heda (1594—1680/82) and Pieter Claesz (1596/97—1661), and *Dessert* by Willem Kalf (1622—1693).

The chief exponents of the animalistic genre was Paulus Potter (1625—1654), the creator of *The Farm*, *The Watch-dog* and *A Bull*, and Aelbert Cuyp (1620—1691).

JACOB VAN RUISDAEL. The Marsh. 1660s

An important part of the exhibition in **room 251** is made up of paintings by Bartholomeus van der Helst (1613—1670), *The Presentation of the Betrothed* and *Family Group*.

Room 254. Rembrandt van Rijn (1606—1669). The Hermitage has twenty-five canvases by Rembrandt, several drawings and sheets of almost all his etchings. There are the *Adoration of the Magi*, a painting only recently identified as a Rembrandt original, and a portrait entitled *The Old Warrior* (*c.* 1629—30). In his search for expressiveness, the young artist here endows his subject with unusual attributes, dressing him in an old beret and the breastplate of a knight The beginning of the 1630s was a period of great success for Rembrandt; he became the best-known painter in Amsterdam. This period is illustrated in the Hermitage

10*

FRANS HALS.
Portrait of a Young Man
with a Glove in His Hand.
Before 1650

by some outstanding works: *Flora*, *Descent from the Cross*, *Abraham's Sacrifice*, *Danaë*, *Parable of the Labourers in the Vineyard* and a number of portraits. The gem of the collection, *Danaë* (1636/46), is based upon a subject that was rather common in the art of the sixteenth and seventeenth centuries, but was interpreted by Rembrandt with freshness and originality. It is not gold, as in the famous painting by Titian, but sunlight pouring in from the depth of the canvas in a warm stream that rushes towards Danaë, illuminating the face of the young woman. Her naked body comes to life, as it were, at the touch of the magic rays. "What a dazzling feast of love!" wrote the Belgian poet Emile Verhaeren of *Danaë*.

In *Flora* Rembrandt portrayed his wife Saskia as the goddess of spring and flowers. She is dressed in a heavy satin garment, and the head of the young woman is crowned with a spray of flowers. The beautiful gold and olive-green colours are characteristic of Rembrandt's work of the 1630s. The main theme in his art is the world of human feelings, and this is seen in canvases painted during different periods and on various subjects. Almost at the same time as *Danaë* Rembrandt painted the *Descent from the Cross* (1634).

The biblical story of the aged Abraham is presented by Rembrandt as an actual event (*Abraham's Sacrifice*, 1635).

The *Parable of the Labourers in the Vineyard* (1637) reflects certain social relationships; the labourers, indignant at an injustice, are presenting their demands to their employer.

Rembrandt's profound realism and the wide scope of his artistic conceptions were alien to his burgher surroundings. At the beginning of the 1640s came the break with official Amsterdam society. Belonging to this period in his work is the small canvas entitled *David's Farewell to Jonathan* (1642), subtle in its psychological mood and priceless in the richness of its artistry. *The Holy Family*, painted in 1645, depicts the Virgin, the Infant Christ and St Joseph as members of the family of a Dutch carpenter. Here kindness, tranquillity and peace reign supreme. Rembrandt's colours in this painting became warmer, a golden red predominating.

The last twenty years of Rembrandt's life—the most mature period of his work—are represented in the Hermitage by a number of portraits and two pictures, *David and Uriah* and the *Return of the Prodigal Son*. In the latter Rembrandt uses the Gospel parable of the reckless youth who leaves his father's house and gives himself up to riotous living, returning home repentant after many ordeals. Rembrandt portrays the emotions experienced by father and son with restraint, but with moving sincerity. Rembrandt's humanity, his ardent belief in man and in the great, ennobling power of love receive here their fullest expression. Both the bold handling and the warm crimson colours are in harmony with the concept of the work.

In the Hermitage there are thirteen portraits by Rembrandt illustrating different periods of his work; among these is the early *Portrait of a Scholar* (1631), in which the young artist focuses attention upon a spontaneous movement of his model; *Portrait of a Young Man with a Lace Collar* (1634), an excellent example of a commissioned portrait of the

period when Rembrandt was the favourite of the Amsterdam burghers; the delicate *Portrait of Baartjen Maertensz Doomer* (*c.* 1640); and the late portrait, seemingly woven out of air and light, of the poet Jeremias de Decker (1666), to whom Rembrandt was bound by friendship lasting many years. The finest paintings produced by the great master in this genre, however, are the psychological portraits of the 1650s when the artist's attention was particularly struck by the faces of old people, bearing as it were the wisdom of experience: *Portrait of an Old Man in Red* (*c.* 1652—54), *Portrait of an Old Woman* (1654) and *Portrait of an Old Man* (1654). In these paintings Rembrandt subtly conveys man's inner world. The face and hands are touched with light; the rest—details of dress and of the immediate surroundings—melt away in a warm semi-darkness.

REMBRANDT. Danaë. 1636

The work of some of Rembrandt's pupils, Jacob Backer, Ferdinand Bol, Jan Lievens, Nicolaes Maes, Aert de Gelder and others, is widely represented in **room 253**. This room also contains five paintings by a teacher of Rembrandt, the famous Amsterdam painter Pieter Lastman (1583—1633)—*Abraham on His Way to Canaan, Bathsheba, Abraham and the Three Angels, The Annunciation* and *Midas' Judgement.*

In **rooms 255—257**, which are situated in a gallery alongside the Hanging Garden, there is an additional exhibition of seventeenth and early eighteenth century Dutch painting. Of particular interest is the very large collection of paintings by Philips Wouwerman (1619—1668), a prolific and, at one time, extremely popular artist who painted battle scenes, hunts, cavalcades, pictures of horses, and landscapes. There is also a large display of paintings by artists of the "Italianizing" trend.

German Art: 15th—18th centuries
First floor, rooms 263—268

A large part of the exhibition is devoted to the German Renaissance. In the first room there is an interesting collection of painted wooden sculptures, for example, *Virgin and Child* and *St George the Victorious* by unknown masters of the late fifteenth century, and *Virgin and Child* by Tilman Riemenschneider. A typical example of fifteenth century German art is the sculptural group *Pietà* (terracotta), in which features of the new humanist vision are discernible despite the adherence to medieval convention. These same tendencies can be seen in the diptych *Christ and the Virgin before God the Father* by Hans von Kulmbach (*c.* 1481/82—1522). In the Hermitage there is a splendid collection of German portrait painting from the Renaissance era. This includes, in **room 263,** the *Portrait of a Young Man* by Ambrosius Holbein (*c.* 1498—1520); in **room 264,** the *Portrait of a Man with His Two Sons* and *Portrait of a Lady with Her Daughter,* painted by Barthel Bruyn the Elder (1493—1555); in **room 265,** *Portrait of a Young Man* and *Portrait of a Woman* by Christoph Amberger (after 1500—*c.* 1561); and in **room 266,** *Portrait of an Elderly Man* and *Portrait of a Young Woman* by Nicholas Neufchatel (*c.* 1520—1567). Lucas Cranach the Elder (1472—1553) is represented by five paintings. Among these are his *Venus and Cupid, Portrait of a Woman* and *Virgin and Child under the Apple-tree,* which rank with the finest examples of the German art of the Renaissance period (**room 264**).

Rooms 266 and 267. The small collection of seventeenth century German painting contains some interesting examples of different genres. These include the formal *Portrait of a Mongolian Merchant with His Sons* by Daniel Schultz (1615—1683); *Portrait of a Young Man in a Fur Cap* and *Still Life* by Christopher Paudiss (1625—1666), who studied painting under Rembrandt; *Self-portrait* by Jürgen Ovens (1623—1679); and the picture of Johann Heinrich Schönfeldt (1609—1679)—*The Wedding at Cana.*

Room 268. Anton Raffael Mengs (1728—1779) was one of the most celebrated exponents of Neoclassicism, which became established in Germany during the second half of the eighteenth century. A typical

REMBRANDT. Portrait of an Old Man in Red. *C.* 1652 – 54

REMBRANDT. The Return of the Prodigal Son. *C.* 1669

example of his work is the painting *Perseus and Andromeda*. Mengs was also active in the field of portraiture (see his *Self-portrait*), which came to be practised on a large scale in eighteenth century German art. This genre is represented in the exhibition by some splendid canvases, painted by artists who at one time were well-known—Antoine Pesne (1683—1757), Anton Graf (1736—1813), and Johann Friedrich August Tischbein (1750—1812). The work of Angelika Kaufmann (1741—1807), who enjoyed great popularity not only in Germany but also abroad, is illustrated by her *Virgil Reading the* Aeneid *to Octavia and Augustus*.

In **rooms 265—268** there are a great many examples of the work of German craftsmen, who were renowned throughout Europe (wood and ivory carvings).

Western European Porcelain: 18th—20th centuries
First floor, rooms 269—271

The Hermitage's magnificent collection of European porcelain comprises several thousand items. The main part, eighteenth century porcelain, is displayed in **room 271**, the former church of the Winter Palace, decorated by Stasov after the fire of 1837 in the style of Rastrelli. The exhibition includes an exceptionally large collection of Saxon porcelain, the initial creation of which by Johann Friedrich Böttger (1682—1719) in 1709 opened up a new era in European ceramics. There are also some specimens of a reddish brown stone-like substance obtained by Böttger in the course of his experiments, a few early examples produced by the Meissen Factory, set up in 1710, and other items from the period when Meissen was flourishing as a centre of porcelain manufacture. Of particular interest are some bird and animal figures and a sculptural group entitled *Parnassus*, by the famous sculptor Johann Joachim Kändler (1706—1775). Notice especially the large banqueting services, Service of the Order of St Andrew First Called and The Hunting Service, made for the Russian court. The exhibition also contains some typical Meissen dishes in the form of fruits, vegetables and flowers, and valuable examples of porcelain ware made in some of the small German factories, including Höchst, Frankenthal, Nymphenburg and Fürstenberg.

Deserving special note is a large eighteenth century service of Viennese porcelain and the Service with the Cameos, consisting of over seven hundred pieces and made to the order of Catherine II in the French town of Sèvres.

The outstanding item in **room 269** is the large dessert set made in Berlin and presented by the Prussian king Frederick the Great to the Russian empress Catherine II in 1722. The purely decorative objects in the set include a large number of figures representing the different nationalities in Russia who are surrounding a throne upon which sits Catherine II. The groups of bound captives and the trophies refer to a Russian victory in the war with Turkey, which lasted from 1768 to 1774.

English Art: 17th—19th centuries
First floor, rooms 298—302

The small collection in the Hermitage enables us to trace the major lines of development in English art, which reached its highest peak in the eighteenth century.

Room 298. 17th and early 18th century art. During this period the main genre in English painting was the portrait. Of the seventeenth century artists represented in the exhibition, Robert Walker (*Portrait of Oliver Cromwell*) and Peter Lely (*Portrait of an English Lady*) continued the tradition of the formal portraits of Van Dyck. Godfrey Kneller (1646—1723) showed greater individuality in his painting; his works include the *Portrait of John Locke* and *Portrait of the Sculptor Grinling Gibbons*. The display includes an excellent collection of seventeenth and eighteenth century English silverware, and there is also in the room the large tapestry *The Wonderful Catch* woven from a cartoon by Raphael at the Mortlake Works in the first half of the seventeenth century.

Room 299. 18th century art. The most outstanding English painter of the eighteenth century was Joshua Reynolds (1723—1792). His large-scale canvas *The Infant Heracles Strangling the Serpents*, commissioned by Catherine II and painted between 1786 and 1788, is an allegorical representation of Russia vanquishing her enemies. *Cupid Untying the Zone of Venus*, also painted by Reynolds, is an example of the mythological

GAINSBOROUGH. Portrait of the Duchess of Beaufort (?). 1770s

Pendant: "The Swan".
Pearl, gold, enamel.
Germany, 16th century

portrait, which at that time was very common. Under Reynolds's influence developed the work of George Romney (1734—1802), a portrait painter popular among London high society (see his *Portrait of Mrs Greer*).

Room 300. Reynolds's great contemporary Thomas Gainsborough (1727—1788), a painter of lyrical landscapes and a distinguished portrait artist, is represented in the Soviet Union by one delightful picture, known as the *Portrait of the Duchess of Beaufort*, painted in the 1770s. The delicate silvery blue range of colours in which the picture was painted emphasizes the refined, exalted beauty of the model. John Hoppner (*Portrait of Sheridan*) and the Scot Henry Raeburn (*Portrait of Eleanor Bethune*) were among the best-known portrait painters of the eighteenth century. In his *Approaching Storm*, George Morland (1763—1804) created a typical eighteenth century English landscape, imbued with a keen perception of nature and enveloped in a mood of romanticism. Also by Morland are the small genre scenes *Gypsies*, *Peasant at a Window* and *The Fish Seller*.

LUCAS CRANACH THE ELDER. The Virgin and Child under the Apple-tree

MORLAND. Approaching Storm. 1791

The Hermitage possesses an unusually large collection of English ceramics, the appearance of which is associated with the name of Josiah Wedgwood (1730—1795). The articles produced in the factory he founded, a new type of unglazed pottery in pale blue, violet and black with white, classical-style relief designs, became widely known in Europe. The "Green Frog" service, made at the Wedgwood factory in 1774 for Catherine II, consists of nine hundred and fifty-two pieces ornamented with English landscape scenes. The small shield containting the representation of a green frog painted on each piece gave the service its name.

Room 301. 19th century art. The English painting of the first half of the nineteenth century is illustrated by the work of such important portrait painters as Thomas Lawrence (1769—1830), George Dawe (1781—1829) and Richard Parkes Bonington (1801/2—1828).

BONINGTON. Boats at a Shore. *C.* 1825

Room 302. The last room of the English exhibition contains individual examples of the art of the second half of the nineteenth century. One item of interest is the large tapestry *The Adoration of the Magi* made from a drawing by Edward Burne-Jones (1833—1898), who belonged to the pre-Raphaelite movement which sprang up in England in the 1840s.

French Art: 15th—18th centuries
First floor, rooms 272—297

The collection of French art in the Hermitage is exceptionally rich and is the finest outside France among the museums of the world. More than forty rooms are used to house the displays of painting, sculpture and various items of applied art.

GOUJON.
Venus and Cupid

Rooms 273 and 274. 15th—16th century art. At the end of the fifteenth century the separate feudal provinces were united into a single French state governed by the king. Within the framework of this national state there developed conditions favourable to the growth of culture. In the town of Limoges the production of enamels was revived after a long interval of time, not *champlevé* as in the Middle Ages (see p. 106) but painted. The very rich collection in the Hermitage allows us to trace the development of the style of fifteenth and sixteenth century French enamellers. Religious subjects were gradually replaced by mythological ones, medieval convention gave way to a realistic handling of themes, and grisaille (a painting executed entirely in monochrome, in a series of greys) superseded polychrome painting, thus making it possible to convey volume, both of figures and of space. The Renaissance artists turned from objects connected with religious worship to the creation of decorative secular articles, such as dishes, jugs and plates.

Room 274. Sixteenth century French court art, the so-called Fontainebleau school, developed under the significant influence of Italian Mannerism. The *Venus and Cupid* relief was created by one of the leading representatives of the Fontainebleau school, Jean Goujon (1510—1568). The sculptor has skilfully worked into his composition, carved on an

LOUIS LE NAIN. The Milkwoman's Family. 1640s

oval medallion, the graceful, somewhat elongated figure of the goddess presented in a fanciful pose. The distinctive originality of sixteenth century French art is seen more clearly in portrait painting. One of the finest items in the exhibition is the *Portrait of the Duke of Alençon*, painted by the famous François Clouet (1520—1572) who was court painter to four French kings.

In a large cabinet there are some faiences by Bernard Palissy (1510—1589), the inventor of a coloured, transparent glazing which gave pottery additional beauty and durability. At one time his decorative dishes with relief designs of fish, snakes and crayfish were tremendously popular; this was called Palissy's rustic pottery. In a case by the windows there are

11 *

three exquisite sixteenth century faience vessels made in the small French town of Saint-Porchaire. They have been preserved up to the present day only as separate items, not as part of a set.

Rooms 275—278. Early and mid-17th century art. During the seventeenth century a number of different trends developed in French art. Two paintings by Simon Vouet (1590—1649), *Heracles among the Olympians* and *Portrait of Anne of Austria as Minerva*, are typical examples of court art at the time of Louis XIII **(room 275)**. **Room 276** contains some of the work of Jacques Callot (1592—1635), a good representative of the realist trend in the French art of this period. A series of etchings produced by him called *The Disasters of War* constitute, for those times, an unusually bold exposure of the bloody events of the Thirty Years' War. Views of Paris and Nancy, prints portraying beggars, gypsies and actors of Italian comedy all point to the great range of this etcher's fine work. Of great importance in seventeenth century French art was the work of the Le Nain brothers, who portrayed peasant life with great sympathy and respect for the common man. *The Milkowan's Family* was painted by Louis (1593—1648), the most talented of the brothers. Also in this room are *Peasants at Table* by Antoine Le Nain and *A Peasant Family* by the third brother, Mathieu.

Room 279. The Hermitage has a very large and valuable collection of the works of Nicolas Poussin (1594—1665), the founder of Neoclassicism in seventeenth century French painting. In the centre of Poussin's vision stands Man, endowed with reason, will and spiritual beauty. Such are the heroes of his numerous paintings on biblical, mythological and literary themes: the selfless Erminia in *Tancred and Erminia*, the fearless Esther of *Esther before Ahasuerus*, and Moses the wise tribal chief in *Moses Striking the Rock*. Poussin's rationalism and philosophical outlook are revealed in his delightful *Landscape with Polythemus* (1649).

Room 280. Claude Lorrain (1600—1682) was a leading exponent of the classical landscape. Composed according to the rules of Classicism, his famous series *The Four Times of the Day* (*Morning*, *Noon*, *Evening* and *Night*) reflects the artist's interest in light, which was something new for French art.

Room 281. Late 17th century art. The official art of France during the golden age of the absolute monarchy served the task of glorifying

POUSSIN. Tancred and Erminia. 1630s

Louis XIV. Artistic life was regulated by the Academy, at the head of which was the *premier peintre* to the king, Charles Lebrun (1619—1690), and after him Pierre Mignard (1612—1695). Mignard's work is represented by the monumental *Magnanimity of Alexander the Great*; in the figure of Alexander is glorified *le roi soleil*, Louis XIV. If Mignard extolled the king in the figure of the great military leader, the sculptor François Girardon (1628—1715) portrayed Louis as a Roman emperor. Girardon's small bronze model for the unpreserved equestrian monument presents the king in the attire of the ancient Roman soldier and in a wig, such as was worn in the seventeenth century.

In **room 282** there is a unique collection of seventeenth and eighteenth century Western European silver, for the most part French. **Rooms 290—297** contain items of French applied art, including furniture, Gobelin tapestries, faience, bronze and porcelain. This collection is

WATTEAU. A Capricious
Woman. *C.* 1718

known throughout the world on account of its exceptional wealth and
because of the great range of items.

Room 283. This exhibition introduces the visitor to the French
portrait painting of the second half of the seventeenth century. The
eminent artist Nicolas Largillière (1656—1746) is represented by a sketch
for a large painting which has not been preserved—a group portrait of
the members of the Paris parliament entitled *Preparation for a Fête in the
Paris Town Hall to Celebrate Louis XIV's Recovery.* The *Portrait of a
Scholar* was painted by the distinguished portrait artist Hyacinthe Rigaud
(1659—1743). The two ebony cupboards, decorated with bronze and
tortoise-shell and used for keeping medals in and were made in the workshop of André-Charles Boulle (1642—1732), a well-known furniture-
maker. An original Boulle cupboard can be seen in **room 293.**

BOUCHER. Pastoral Scene. 1740s

Rooms 284—289. 18th century art. This room contains several pieces by one of France's most eminent artists, Antoine Watteau (1684—1721) who, in his search for a realist approach, broke with hidebound academic convention. In his small paintings *The Hardships of War* and *The Recreations of War* **(room 284)** Watteau portrayed the everyday life of a soldier rather than ostentatious battle scenes as his predecessors had done. The *Savoyard with a Marmot* (1716), a picture of a simple-hearted young travelling musician, also confirms Watteau's interest in the simple phenomena of life. The blue expanse of the clear, fresh sky, the buildings of the small town, and the silhouettes of the bare trees make up a landscape in which the fresh colours of autumn are dominant. Watteau became famous after his adoption of a completely new genre, as a painter of so-called *fêtes galantes*. An example of this type of painting

FALCONET. Flora. 1750s

is the *Embarrassing Proposal*, painted around 1716. Some members of fashionable society are amusing themselves chatting in the shade of the gossamery foliage; the casually graceful postures of the young ladies and their admirers convey subtle, almost imperceptible shades of emotion. Exquisite colouring and delicate execution distinguish one of the artist's masterpieces, a small painting *A Capricious Woman* (*c.* 1718), in which the spectator encounters the same world of superficial feelings.

The exhibition in **rooms 285** and **286** presents examples of Rococo court art which existed, according to the apt remark of a contemporary, "in order to please". Venuses, cupids, shepherd boys and shepherd girls are the central figures of the many works of François Boucher (1703— 1770), a court painter of Louis XV. Boucher's *Pastoral Scene*, *The Triumph of Venus* and *The Toilet of Venus*, confined in their colours to

CHARDIN. The Washerwoman. *C.* 1737

attractive pinks and blues, are very typical of Rococo art, of which he was a distinguished exponent.

In **room 285** particular mention should be made of the work of Etienne-Maurice Falconet (1716—1791), who executed the equestrian statue of Peter the Great ("Bronze Horseman") in St Petersburg. His *Cupid* and *Flora*, in which elegance is combined with the true-to-life quality of the figures, are evidence of the sculptor's faithful adherence to realist traditions. In a large cabinet by the window, among some Sèvres porcelains, are the unglazed white porcelain (biscuit) statuettes *Cupid*, *Psyche* and *Woman Bathing*, made from models of Falconet.

Room 286 contains a number of portraits by Jean-Marc Nattier and Louis Tocqué, painters who at one time enjoyed considerable popularity. Falconet's sculpture *Winter* is distinguished from his earlier works by its

HOUDON. Voltaire. 1781

greater severity of style; this is related to the growing influence of Classicism in French art during the last thirty years or so of the eighteenth century.

Room 287. Jean-Baptiste-Siméon Chardin (1699—1779) was a leading representative of the realist movement. His *Washerwoman* (*c.* 1737) and *Grace before Meat* (1744) take the onlooker into the sphere of activities and everyday problems and chores of a poor French family. Chardin was an outstanding painter of still life, which was unknown to French aristocratic art as an independent genre. The appeal of the *Still Life with the Attributes of the Arts*, painted by Chardin in 1766 for the St Petersburg Academy of Fine Arts, lies in the austere conception of the composition and the subtle, skilful use of colour.

The centre of the room is occupied by the marble statue of the great man of the Enlightenment, Voltaire (1781), created by the realist sculptor Jean-Antoine Houdon (1741—1828).

Also of interest are the portrait busts of Diderot and Falconet carved in marble by Marie-Anne Collot (1748—1821).

Room 288. The painting *Paralytic Helped by His Children*, one of the most famous canvases by Jean-Baptiste Greuze (1725—1805), was considered to be an affirmation of bourgeois virtue and a protest against the depravity of the aristocracy and the frivolity of Rococo art. Another example of this type of moralizing scene is his painting *Widow Visiting the Curé*. Greuze's artistic merit is seen fully in such works as *The Spoilt Child*, *Girl with a Doll* and *Young Man in a Hat*.

Three paintings—*The Stolen Kiss*, *The Farmer's Children* and *The Snatched Kiss*—illustrate the work of the fine painter of the second half of the eighteenth century Jean-Honoré Fragonard (1732—1806). There are also some paintings by the famous landscape painter Claude Joseph Vernet (1714—1789).

Room 289. In the White Room (designed by Briullov, 1838) there are paintings, sculptures and items of applied art from the last thirty years of the eighteenth century. During these years Hubert Robert (1733—1808) enjoyed great popularity; ancient ruins were the favourite theme of his decorative landscapes.

French Art: 19th—20th centuries
Second floor, rooms 314—333, 343—350

Room 314. A new chapter in French history was opened in 1789 when the feudal Bourbon monarchy collapsed. The artistic movement which expressed the revolutionary aspirations of the progressive factions of French society was Neoclassicism. The *Death of Cato of Utica* by Guillaume Lethière (1760—1832) gives us some idea of the distinctive features of this movement. Cato, a confirmed Republican, commits suicide upon hearing of the establishment of Caesar's dictatorship.

During the First Empire artists began to choose idyllic or allegorical themes. Guérin's paintings *Morpheus and Iris* and *Sapho* and two

sculptures, Chaudet's *Cypress* and Canova's *Dancer*, illustrate the fundamental changes in Neoclassical art.

The leading figure in French Neoclassicism was Jacques-Louis David
(1748—1825). From his late canvas *Sapho and Phaon* (1809) it is evident
that at the time of the Empire no traces remained of the revolutionary
spirit of the former member of the National Convention, the creator of
the *Death of Marat*.

In the same room is Antoine Gros's (1771—1835) *Napoleon upon the
Bridge at Arcole*. This painting is based upon the actual event at the time
of the Italian campaign of 1797; during the battle of Arcole Bonaparte,
a young general at that time, was the first to rush forward and, leading his
men, began the assault on the bridge.

In the *Portrait of Josephine* (Napoleon's first wife) François Gérard
(1770—1837) presents a new type of formal portrait, in which he skilfully

DUPRÉ. Forest Scene

combines the austerity of a classical composition with a simple and unaffected rendering of the appearance of his model. One of the first artists
to portray the everyday life of the bourgeois society of his time was
Louis Boilly, who painted the small picture *A Game of Billiards*.

Room 331. Eugène Delacroix (1798—1863), the major painter of the
Romantic movement, is represented in the Hermitage by two late works,
Lion Hunt in Morocco (1854) and *Arab Saddling His Horse* (1855). Painted
in bright, fresh colours, Delacroix's canvases are filled with the ardent
breath of life, and a sense of grandeur of nature.

One of the representatives of the Romantic movement in sculpture is
the animalist Antoine Barye (1796—1875), the creator of the bronze
groups *A Lion and a Snake* and *A Panther and an Antelope*. Barye imbues
his works with great expressiveness, revealing in them the harsh laws of
the animal kingdom.

RENOIR. Girl with a Fan. 1881

Jean-Dominique Ingres (1780—1867) was among the most subtle and complex artists of the mid-nineteenth century. The only painting by him in the Hermitage is the portrait of the Russian diplomat Count Guryev, painted in 1821 and notable for the austere formal arrangement and the strength and assurance of line.

Rooms 321, 322, 325, 328 and 329. There is a large collection of landscapes of the Barbizon school in the Hermitage. Its leading figure, Théodore Rousseau (1812—1867), showed, even in one of his early works *In the Vicinity of Granville*, that the simple, visually unprepossessing countryside of Normandy could become a source of inspiration. Close to Rousseau in their perception of nature are Jules Dupré, Charles François Daubigny, Diaz de la Peña, Charles Jacque and Constant Troyon.

RENOIR. Portrait of the Actress Jeanne Samary. 1878

DEGAS.
Woman Combing
Her Hair. 1886

An important place in the history of French landscape painting belongs to Camille Corot (1796—1875). Corot did not strive for an accurate reproduction of landscape. His poetic landscapes are echoes of the artist's own experiences.

The work of the leading painters of the realist movement, Jean-François Millet (1814—1875) and Gustave Courbet (1819—1877), developed in the 1850s—1860s. Millet was the first among his contemporaries to depict French village life, with what was then unusual degree of profundity and veracity. The Hermitage possesses only one of his paintings, *Peasant Women Carrying Firewood*.

The only Courbet in the Hermitage is the *Landscape with a Dead Horse* which does not give us any real idea of his skill as an artist.

Room 320. Towards the 1870s Impressionism reached its peak in France, the movement having originated as a protest against the rigid

RODIN.
Eternal Spring.
After 1884

convention which prevailed in official art. The Impressionists emerged as
heirs to the realist traditions and enriched painting with their fresh,
joyful colours, their representation of light, and exquisite rendering of
atmosphere. They drew only from life capturing the spontaneity and
naturalness of the first visual impression. In conveying the wealth of
colour in the real world around them the Impressionists attempted
to catch and to record its face, forever changing under the play
of light.

Auguste Renoir (1841—1919) embodies the principles and methods of
Impressionism in portrait painting. Renoir did not attempt to reveal in
his portraits intricate feelings or emotions; he caught the spontaneous
movement, the half-smile, the gentle reverie of his model. Unaffected
animation and simplicity characterize his *Girl with a Fan* and *Portrait
of the Actress Jeanne Samary*. Renoir's colours are notable for their

MONET. Lady in a Garden. 1860s

freshness, the richness of hues, and the extremely delicate transition from one tone to the next.

The work of Edgar Degas (1834—1917) is represented by some pastels —*Woman Combing Her Hair*, *After the Bath* and *Dancers' Heads*. Together with the Impressionist paintings are displayed marble sculptures by Auguste Rodin (1840—1917) and bronzes by Aristide Maillol (1861—1942).

Room 319. One of the leading Impressionist painters was Claude Monet (1840—1925). An early work of his, *Lady in the Garden* (1860s), reflects the first success of the new manner of painting. Abandoning black and subdued tones, Monet painted the shade in colour depending on the surrounding milieu. The woman's white dress in the shade of

VAN GOGH. Cottages with Thatched Roofs. 1890

the parasol, for example, acquires a bluish hue against the background of the green foliage and the blue sky. In the landscapes *River Bank* (1873) and *London Fog* (1903), the canvas is filled as it were with the subtle, barely perceptible movement of currents of moist air, in which outlines of things melt into nothing.

Room 318. Paris street life with its characteristic bustle, commotion and endless flow of traffic and pedestrians was captured by Camille Pissarro (1830—1903) in his magnificent paintings *The Boulevard Montmartre à Paris* and *La Place du Théâtre Français à Paris*.

The eleven paintings by Paul Cézanne (1839—1906) make it possible to observe the main stages in the development of the artist's work. Unlike the Impressionists Cézanne tried to reveal the materiality and plasticity

GAUGIN.
Woman Holding a Fruit. 1893

of whatever he depicted. Typical in this way is the landscape *Banks of the Marne* (1888), in which he painted a tranquil scene from nature, as though trying to immortalize on canvas her immutable qualities. Still-life painting was Cézanne's favourite genre. His still lifes are simple: a wooden table, two or three faience vessels, some fruit, all these objects possessing some special distinctive corporeity peculiar to Cézanne. To preserve their "eternal" qualities — weight and volume — Cézanne made the form geometric, building it up with thick strokes of bright green, orange and blue.

Room 317. The Hermitage has four paintings by Vincent van Gogh (1853—1890): *View of the Arena in Arles, Ladies of Arles (Memory of the Garden at Etten), Bushes,* and *Cottages with Thatched Roofs,* painted during the last years of the artist's life. Van Gogh's characteristic dra-

MATISSE. The Dance. 1910

matic tension is felt in the vividness of the colours, the restless rhythm of the thick, energetic brushstrokes, and the expressiveness of line.

Displayed in the same room are *Tropical Forest* and the *Luxembourg Gardens with the Bust of Chopin* by Henri Rousseau (1844–1910), usually referred to as a Primitive.

Room 316. The fifteen paintings in the Hermitage by Paul Gauguin (1848–1903) belong to his so-called Tahitian period. In his pictures painted in the tropics Gauguin extolls a world untouched by "civilization" and full of the exotic, where people live in harmony with nature. Gauguin's paintings are decorative, the areas of local colours lie on the canvas in motionless patches, and the contours of the figures and objects, —sometimes smooth and fluid, sometimes exquisitely delicate—give the picture the semblance of a coloured pattern (*Tahitian Pastorals, Woman Holding a Fruit, Miraculous Source, The Idol*, etc.).

Rooms 343—345. The thirty-five pictures by Henri Matisse (1869—1954), painted between 1900 and 1913, make it possible to illustrate the special features of the work of one of the leading twentieth century French artists. *The Family Group*, *Red Room* and other of Matisse's works are striking in their decorative quality and their saturated colours. Rejecting a chiaroscuro treatment, Matisse simplifies and schematizes his figures and objects, building up his composition on the contrasting juxtaposition of large areas of pure colour. The radiant colourfulness of Matisse's canvases produces a feeling of joy and gaiety.

Rooms 346 and 347. Pablo Picasso (1881—1973). The development of Picasso's work is unusually complex and contradictory. The Hermitage collection consisting of thirty-six works helps illustrate just the beginning of this development. In one of the best paintings of his early period, *Woman Drinking Absinth* (1901), Picasso created a type that evokes a deep sense of tragedy. The *Portrait of Soler* and *The Visit (Two Sisters)* belong to the so-called Blue Period (1901—4); his Pink Period (1905—6) is represented by a gouache drawing, *Boy with a Dog*.

Between 1906 and 1907 Picasso was absorbed with analysis of form and reduced everything to a simplified volume similar to a cube, a sphere or a cylinder. He became one of the founders of a new tendency in art, Cubism, typical of which are such works as *Woman with a Fan*, *Three Women*, *Pitcher and Bowl* and others. After this Picasso arrived at a complete break-up of form; he destroys volume and creates free compositions from planes and lines (cf. *Flute and Violin*, 1912). Such experiments only led him to a dead end and he gave up experimenting further.

Rooms 348 and 349. Among the paintings displayed of early twentieth century artists are works by André Derain (1880—1954)—*The Wood*, *The Lake* and *A Harbour in Provence*; Maurice Vlaminck (1876—1958)—*A View of the Seine*; Jean-Edouard Vuillard (1868—1940)—*A Room* and *Children*; Pierre Bonnard (1867—1947)—*The Arrival of Spring* and *A Corner of Paris*; Louis Valtat (1869—1952)—*Pleasure Party in the Garden*; Maurice Denis (1870—1943)—*Spring Landscape with Figures*.

Room 350 contains a large collection of pictures by the fine landscape painter Albert Marquet (1875—1947), whose greatest love was Paris and who painted her streets and squares, embankments and bridges over

PICASSO. Boy with a Dog. 1905

RENATO GUTTUSO.
Rocco and Son. 1960

the Seine. The colours in his landscapes are always true to life and objects are represented in a very generalized way (cf. *Rainy Day in Paris, The Louvre Embankment and the Pont-Neuf in Paris* and *Naples*).

Displayed in the same room are landscapes by Léopold Survage (1879—1968) and André Fougeron (born 1913). *The Bridge* was painted by the latter in 1964. Glowing colouring and great vitality distinguish the *Red Dancer* and *Lady in a Black Hat* by Cornelius Kees Van Dongen (1877—1968).

In **room 350** are also shown paintings by Fernand Léger (1881—1955), —*Carte postale* and *Composition*.

German Art: 19th century
Second floor, rooms 342, 341

An important part of the exhibition in these rooms is occupied by an excellent collection of works by the Romantic landscape painter Caspar David Friedrich (1774—1840), including *Harbour at Night*, *Morning in the Hills* and *On a Sailing Ship*. The paintings of Friedrich Overbach (1789—1869), Alfred Rethel (1816—1859) and Philipp Veit (1793—1877) are characteristic of the so-called Nazarene school, one of the currents in German Romanticism.

The display includes also genre paintings by Ludwig Knaus (1829—1910) and Wilhelm Leibl (1844—1900) and a pastel by Max Liebermann (1847—1935), the principal representative of Impressionism in Germany.

Belgian and Dutch Art: 19th century
Second floor, room 340

Nineteenth century Belgian art is represented by the genre paintings of Joseph Stevens (1819—1892) and Hendrick Leys (1815—1869). They are evidence of the strengthening of realist tendencies in nineteenth century Belgian art. The lightly coloured *After a Walk* by Gustave de Jonghe (1829—1893) illustrates the influence of the French Impressionists upon Belgian artists. The work of the distinguished painter, sculptor and engraver Constantin Meunier (1831—1905), who portrayed the life of the Belgian proletariat, is illustrated by a small bronze relief entitled *The Head of a Miner*.

Nineteenth century Dutch art is represented by Jan Weissenbruch's *Street in a Dutch Town* and by Albert Neuhuijs's *Family of a Cobbler*.

Finnish, German and Spanish Art:
late 19th—early 20th centuries
Second floor, room 339

Much of the work of the eminent realist painter Albert Edelfelt (1854—1905) is based upon themes associated with the life of the Finnish people and with the countryside of his native country (*The Laundresses, Pines in Borga, Fishermen at Sea*). Edelfelt also enjoyed considerable success in the field of portrait painting, an example of which is his *Portrait of M. Geirot*.

The German school is represented by works of Franz Stuck (1863—1929)—*Fight over a Woman* (1905) and Hans Thoma (1839—1924)—*Adam and Eve* (1897).

In this room is also displayed *The Dwarf Gregorio* by the Spanish artist Ignacio Zuloaga (1870—1946).

Italian Art: 20th century
Second floor, room 338

The small collection of paintings by twentieth century Italian artists includes some works of Renato Guttuso (born 1912)—*Rocco and Son* (1960) and *Potatoes on Yellow Paper* (1961). Of particular note are the monumental painting *Seamstresses* by Massimo Campigli (born 1895), the subtly coloured *Still Life* by Giorgio Morandi (1890—1964) and *Flowers* by Filippo de Pisis (1896—1956).

Finnish and Belgian Art: 20th century
Second floor, room 337

Twentieth century Finnish art is represented by *Two Girls* of Juho Rissanen (1873—1950) and *Morning in a Peasant House* by Eero Neli-markka (born 1891). Also of interest is the sketch for the mural *Children* by Henry Ericksson (1898—1933) and the small wooden carvings of the popular sculptor and caricaturist Albin Kaasinen (born 1892)—*Seeing Off* and *In the Sauna*.

Meunier's realist traditions were continued by Roger Somville (born 1923)—*A Miner from Borinage* and Robert Crommelynck (born 1895)—*Peat Worker*. The exhibition is rounded off by the *Old Woman* by Kurt Peiser (1887—1962) and *Self-portrait* by François Depooter (born 1898).

Art of the United States of America:
20th century
Second floor, room 336

The exhibition consists almost entirely of paintings by the famous American artist Rockwell Kent (1882—1971). Kent presented a large collection of his works to the Soviet people and of these twenty-six are in the Hermitage. His landscapes reproduce the unique features of the sombre scenery of the North. The room also contains paintings by Maurice Pass (born 1891), Frank Kirk (born 1896), Alfred Henry (1868—1932) and James Wilson Morrice (1864—1924).

Art of the German Democratic Republic
Second floor, room 335

This room houses a collection of works by artists from the German Democratic Republic, among which can be noted the *Shooting of the Sailor Engelhofer*, a monumental triptych by Heinrich Ehmsen (1886—1963), *Portrait of an Old Worker* by Otto Nagel (1884—1967), and a number of paintings by Hans Grundig (1901—1958).

Czechoslovakian, Hungarian, Polish
and Rumanian Art: 20th century
Second floor, room 334

Exhibited in this room are works by artists from socialist countries in Europe. One ought to single out *Wet Snow* by the Hungarian artist Mohasci (born 1924), *A View of the Tatras* by the Polish painter Rafat Malczewski (born 1892), *Composition* by the Polish artist Romuald Witkowski (1876—1950), *Three Odalisques* by Joseph Iser (1881—1958, Rumania) and *Still Life* by Vincent Beneš (born 1883, Czechoslovakia).

Western European Tapestry:
15th—18th centuries
First floor, room 303
(The Dark Passage)

The Hermitage collection of Western European tapestries—wall carpets woven on hand looms from woolen and silk threads—is among the finest in the world.

Deserving particular attention are the rare examples of sixteenth century Netherlandish tapestries from the series *The History of the Knight of the Swan* and *Roman de la Rose*, seventeenth century Flemish tapestries made after cartoons by Rubens and pupils of his, and eighteenth century French gobelins from the series *The History of Esther* and *The Golden Fleece*. Beautiful examples can also be seen in the exhibition of Netherlandish art **(room 260)**, French art **(rooms 290—297)** and English art **(room 298)**, in the Alexander Room **(282)** and in the tapestry corridor **(200** and **201)**.

Western European Carved Stone:
12th—19th centuries
First floor, room 304

The Hermitage collection comprises more than ten thousand intaglios and cameos made by craftsmen from Western European countries. The exhibition is housed in the Gilt Drawing-room of the Winter Palace, decorated in 1853 by the architect Schreiber.

Western European Jewellery:
16th—19th centuries

The **Gold Room** contains a superb collection of jewellery including the work of jewellers from France, England, Germany, Italy, Spain, Switzerland, Holland, Sweden, and Denmark, and of foreign craftsmen who worked in Russia. Exceptional for its wealth and diversity, the exhibition—including pendants, rings, snuff-boxes, sprays made of precious stones, watches, perfume bottles, needle boxes, walking sticks and caskets—enables us to trace the development of styles in jewellery from the sixteenth up to the nineteenth century.

THE NUMISMATIC DEPARTMENT

This department contains unique collections of antique, oriental, European and Russian coins, as well as medals, decorations and badges. The items from this collection are included in the exhibitions of all the departments in the Hermitage. **Rooms 398—400** house a special exhibition of decorations and badges.

FLOOR PLANS

GROUND FLOOR

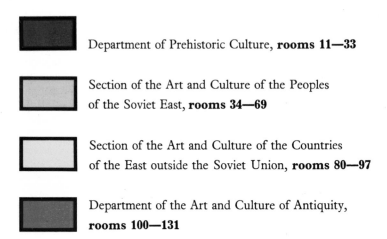

Department of Prehistoric Culture, **rooms 11—33**

Section of the Art and Culture of the Peoples
of the Soviet East, **rooms 34—69**

Section of the Art and Culture of the Countries
of the East outside the Soviet Union, **rooms 80—97**

Department of the Art and Culture of Antiquity,
rooms 100—131

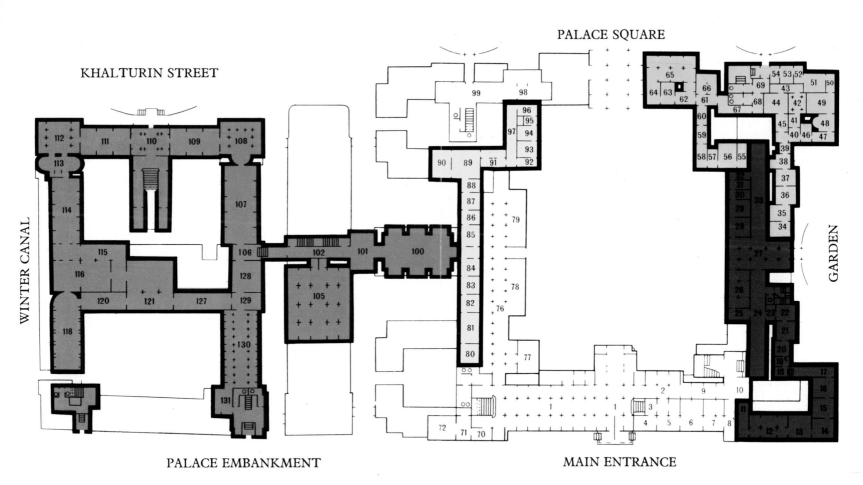

PALACE SQUARE

KHALTURIN STREET

WINTER CANAL

GARDEN

PALACE EMBANKMENT

MAIN ENTRANCE

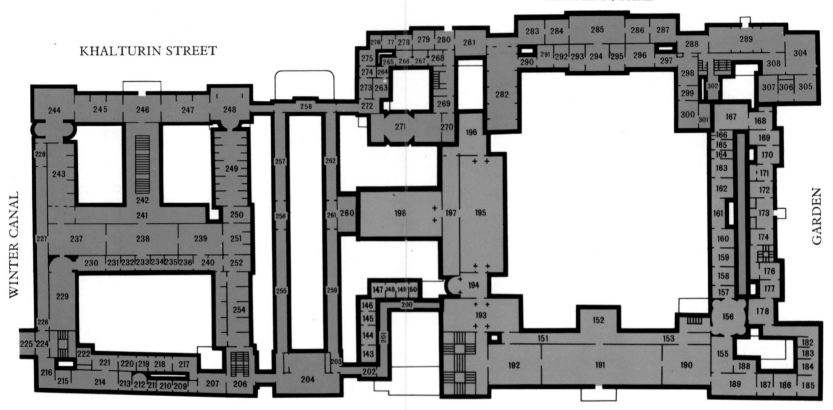

PALACE SQUARE

KHALTURIN STREET

WINTER CANAL

GARDEN

PALACE EMBANKMENT

1st FLOOR

 Department of Ruissian Culture, **rooms 143—198**

 Department of Western European Art, **rooms 200—308**

2nd FLOOR

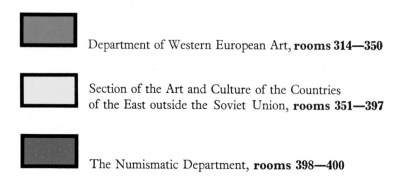

Department of Western European Art, **rooms 314—350**

Section of the Art and Culture of the Countries of the East outside the Soviet Union, **rooms 351—397**

The Numismatic Department, **rooms 398—400**

PALACE SQUARE

SMALL HERMITAGE

GARDEN

PALACE EMBANKMENT

CONTENTS

Frontispiece:

The Malachite Room. Winter Palace

Olga Persianova
THE HERMITAGE
Room-to-room guide
Third edition, revised

Ольга Михайловна Персианова
ГОСУДАРСТВЕННЫЙ ЭРМИТАЖ
Краткий путеводитель
Издание 3-е, исправленное

Перевод Дж. Хейса
Оформление художника В. В. Бабанова
Редактор М. Ю. Ралль
Редактор английского текста Э. Г. Андреева
Художественный редактор Е. Б. Большаков
Технический редактор В. Л. Иванова
Корректор И. Н. Стукалина

Подписано в печать 17/I 1976. Формат
70 × 103 1/32, бумага мелованная. Усл. печ. л.
8,75. Уч.-изд. л. 9,92. Тираж 50 000.
Изд. № 1846. (1-32). Издательство „Аврора“,
191065, Ленинград, Невский пр., 7/9
Издано в СССР